Flower Mandalas
coloring book
Volume 1

Illustrated by

Pamela Duarte

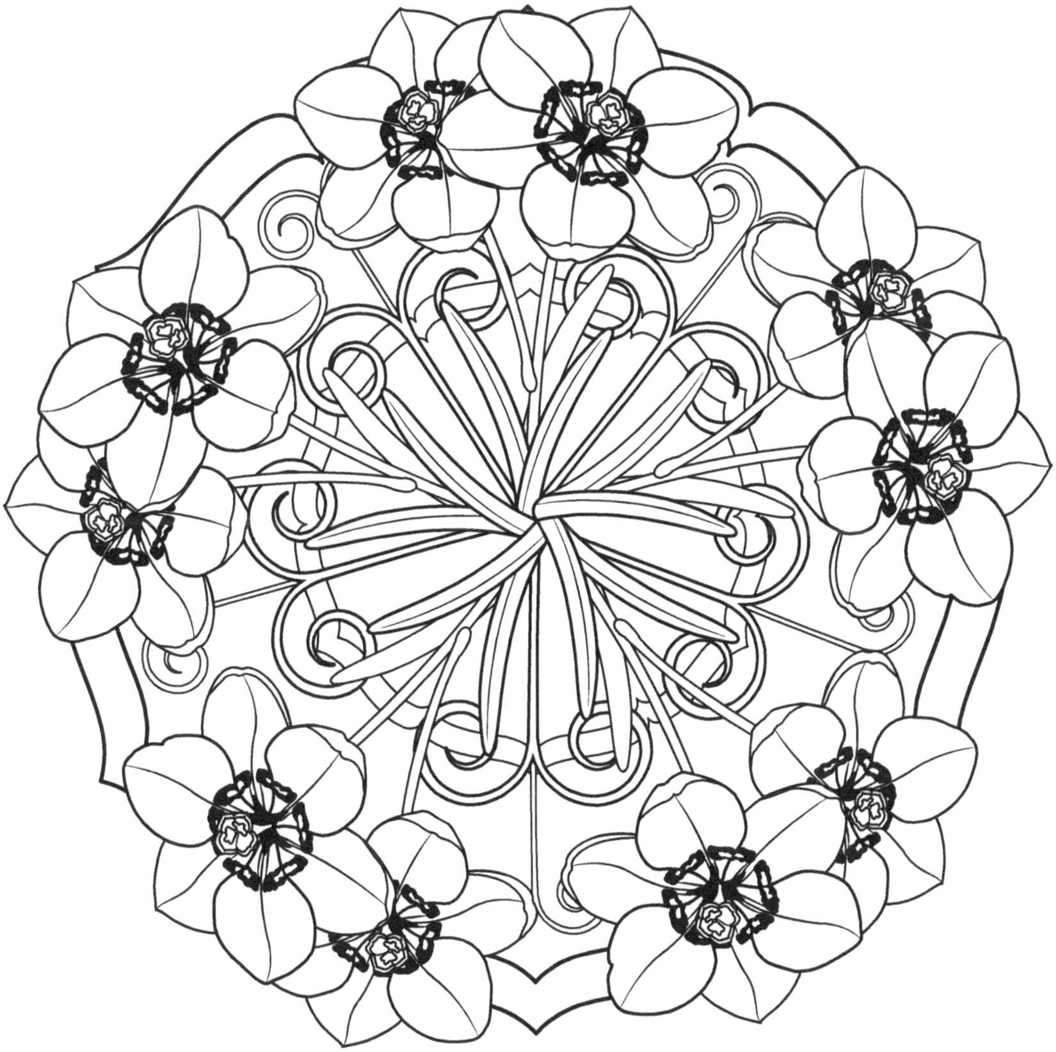

I0484014

Flower Mandalas Coloring Book, Volume 1
©2015 Pamela Duarte

I have created coloring books for other clients in my career as a professional illustrator but for a long time have wanted to illustrate a book in which I could create the subject matter on my own. I love flowers and the natural world and so chose that as the inspiration for this book. If you love flowers too, please collaborate with me!

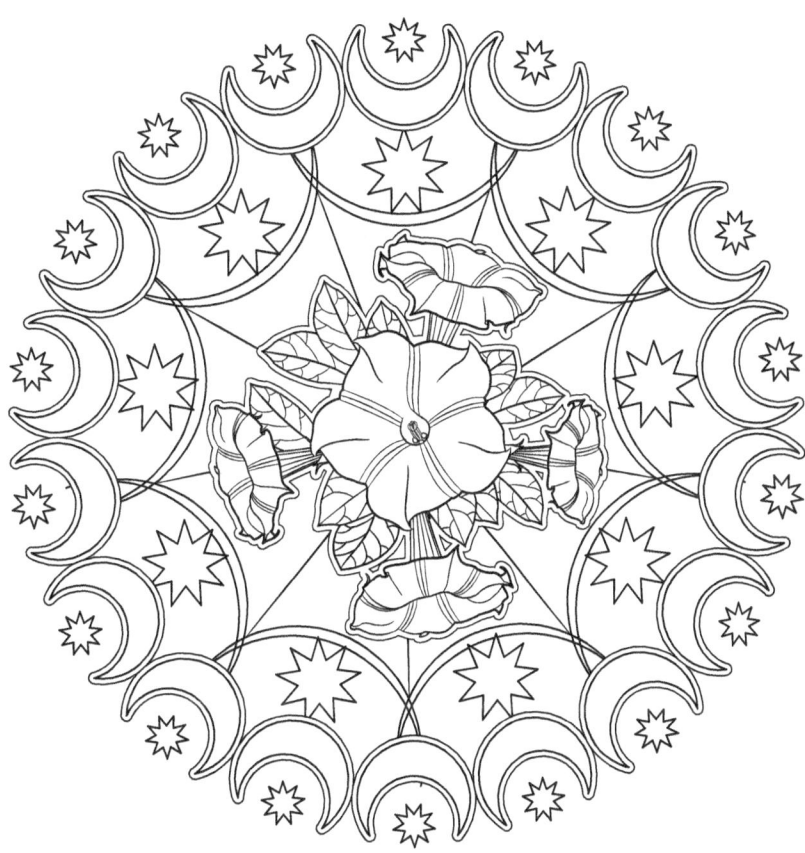

This book is dedicated to 3 strong women:

My Mother who has always been supportive of my goals,
My Grandmother who taught me to appreciate beauty,
and to
Carolee Bingham who loved to color mandalas
& who inspired this book.

The pages of this book are suitable for colored pencils, markers, and a variety of other media. They are only printed on one side and to help prevent bleed through, please place a blank sheet of paper between the pages when coloring.

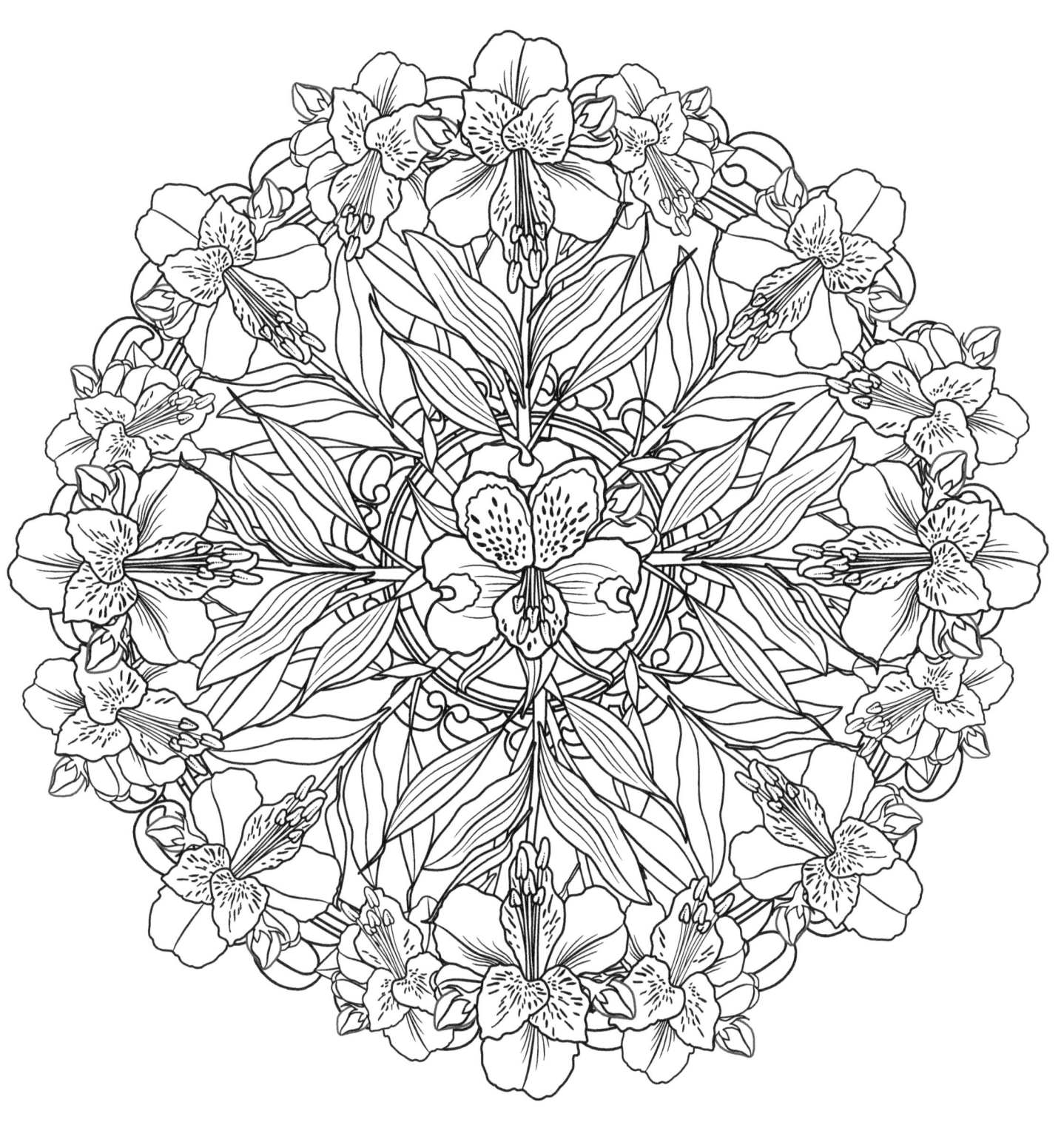

Peruvian Lily
Alstroemeria

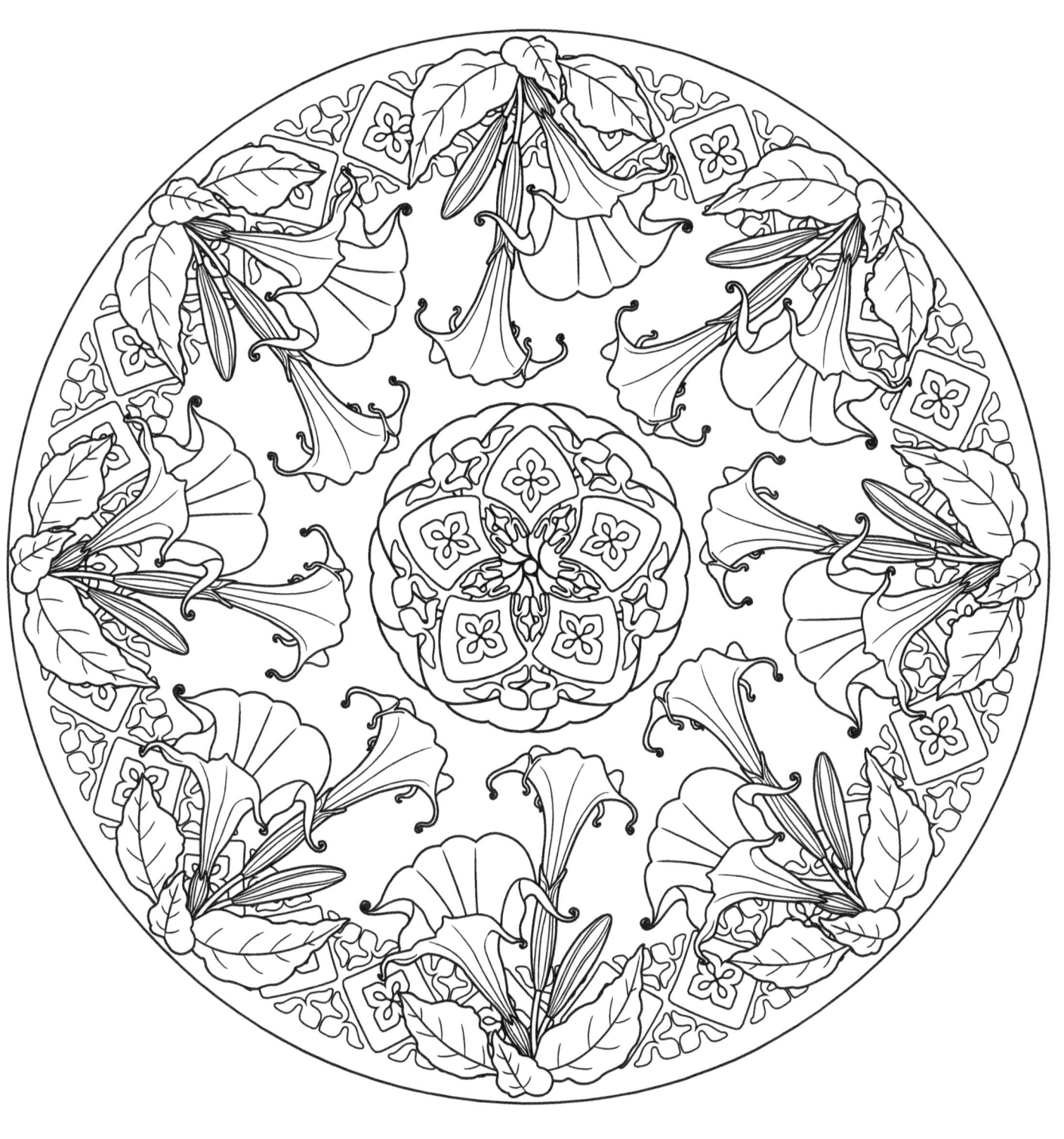

Angel's Trumpet
Brugmansia

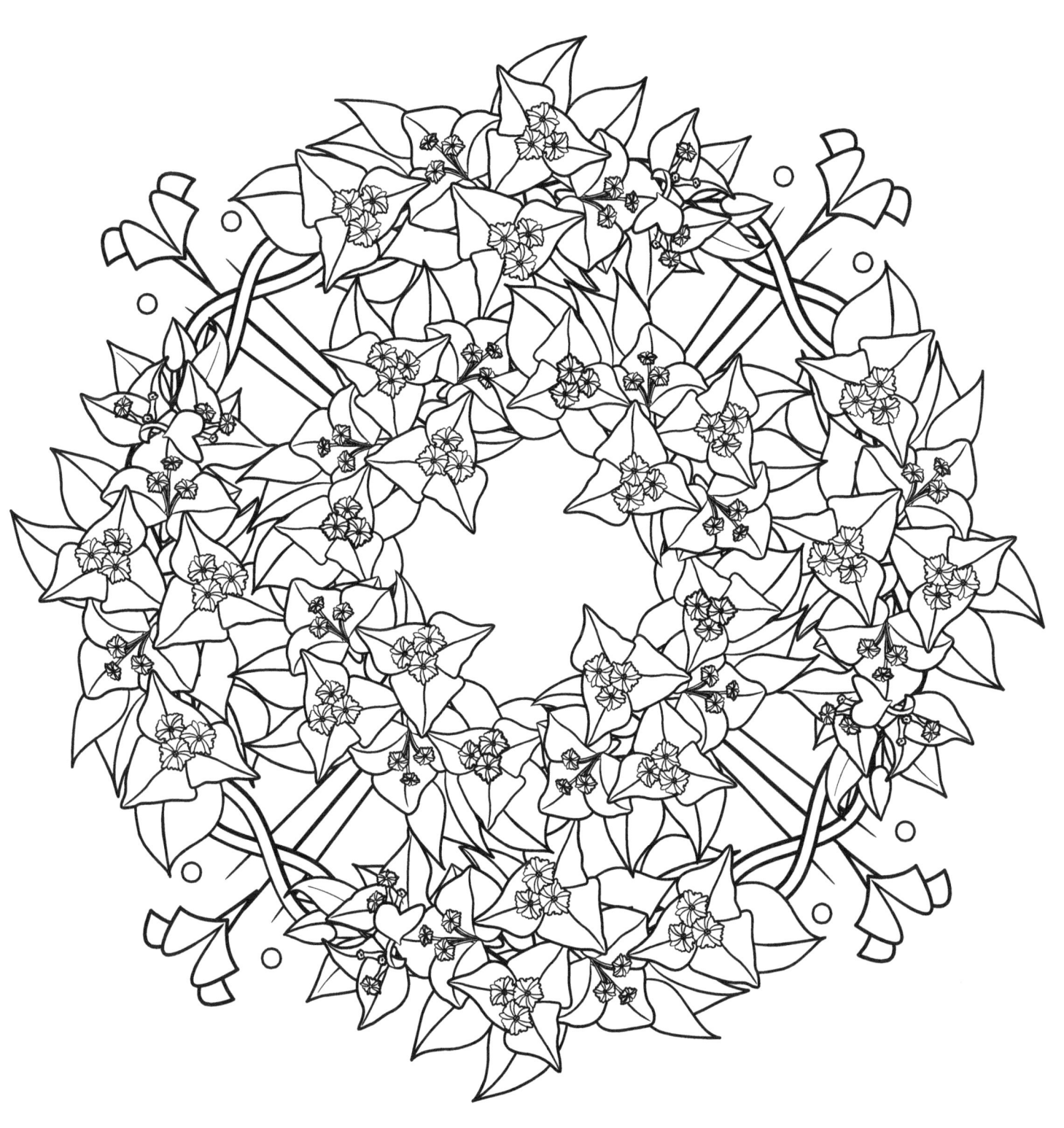

Bougainvillea
Bougainvillea glabra

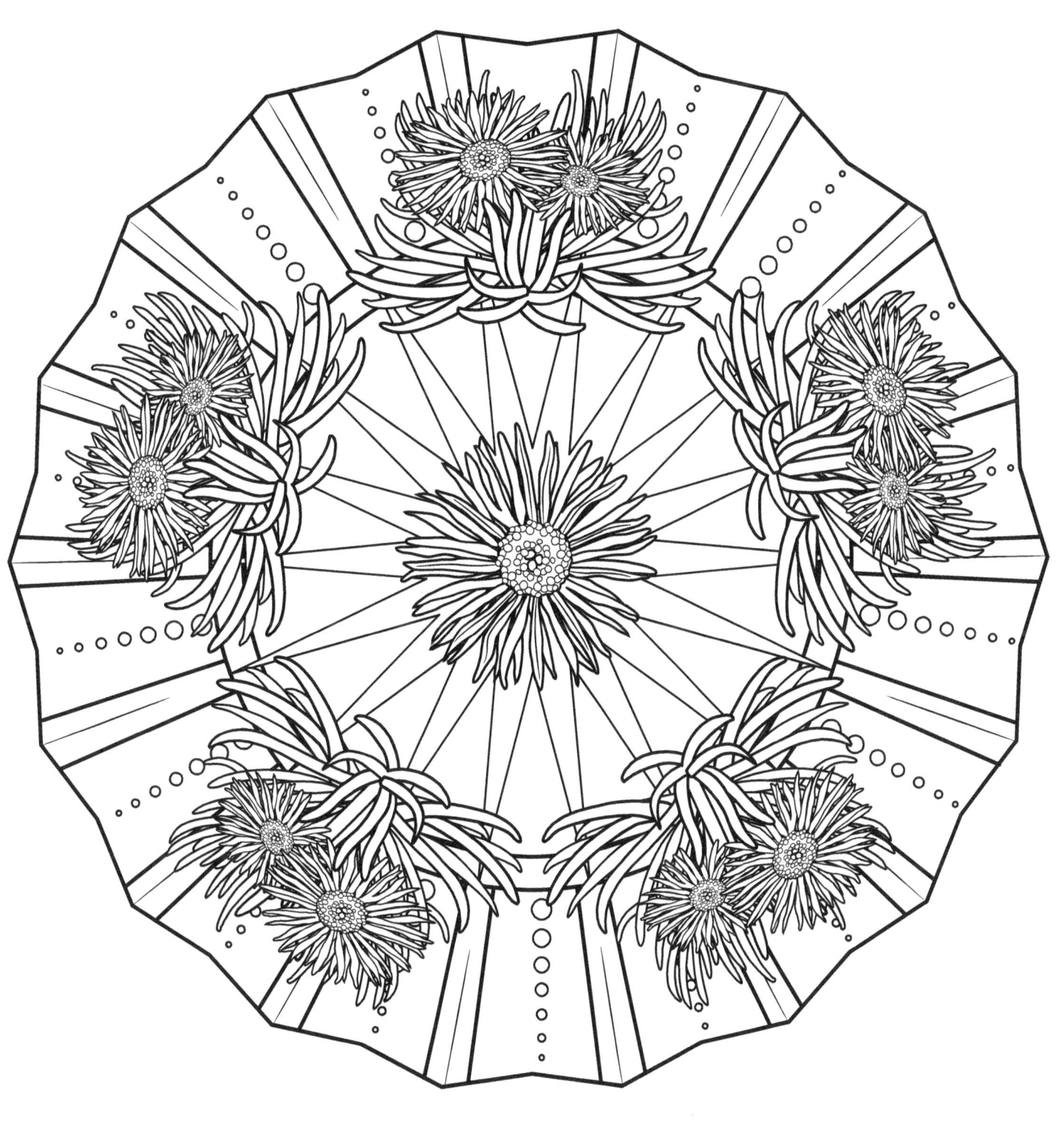

African Ice Plant
Cephalopyllum Pillansii

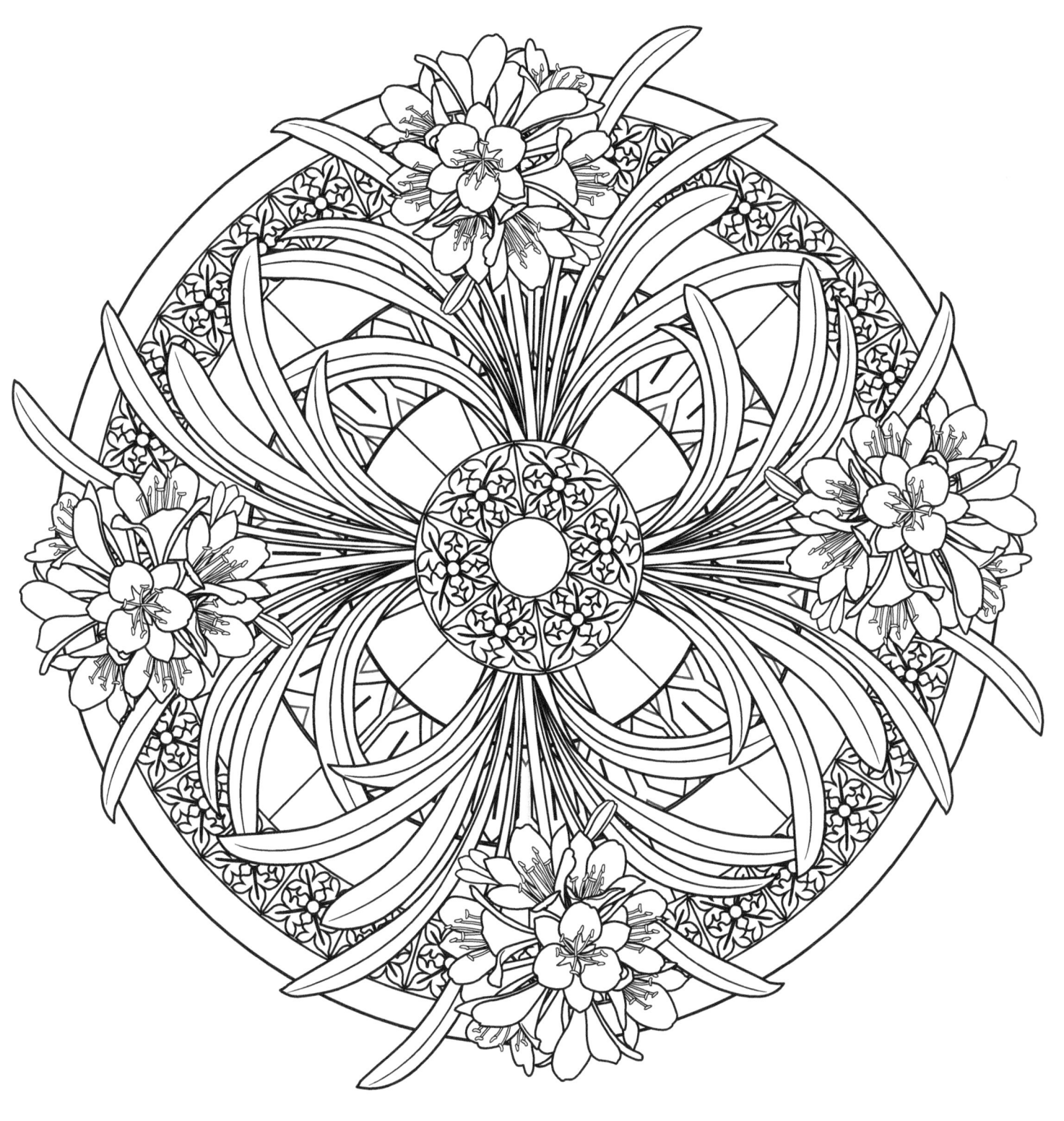

Clivia
Amaryllidaceae

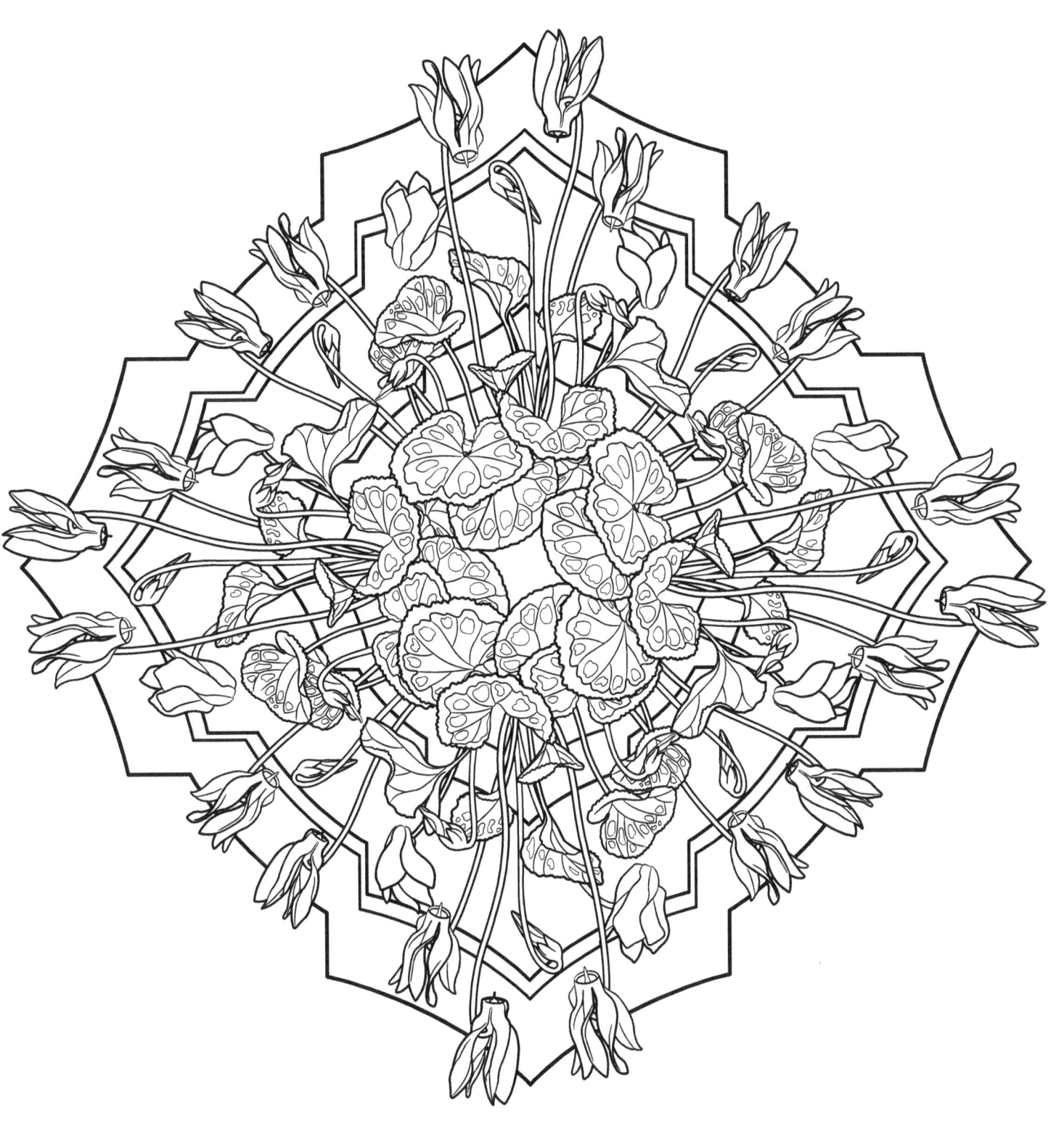

Cyclamen
Primulaceae

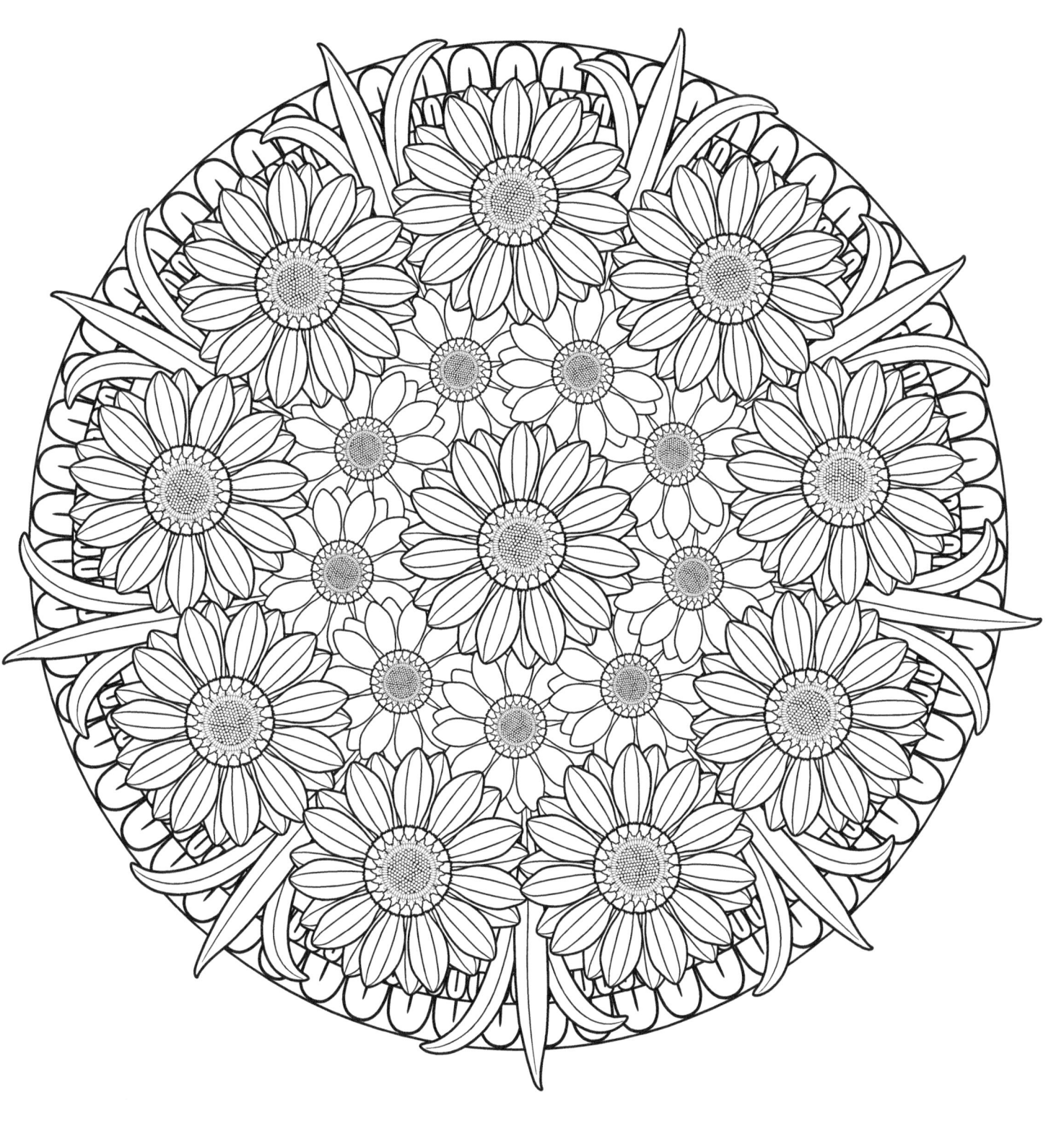

Gazania
Gazania Splendens

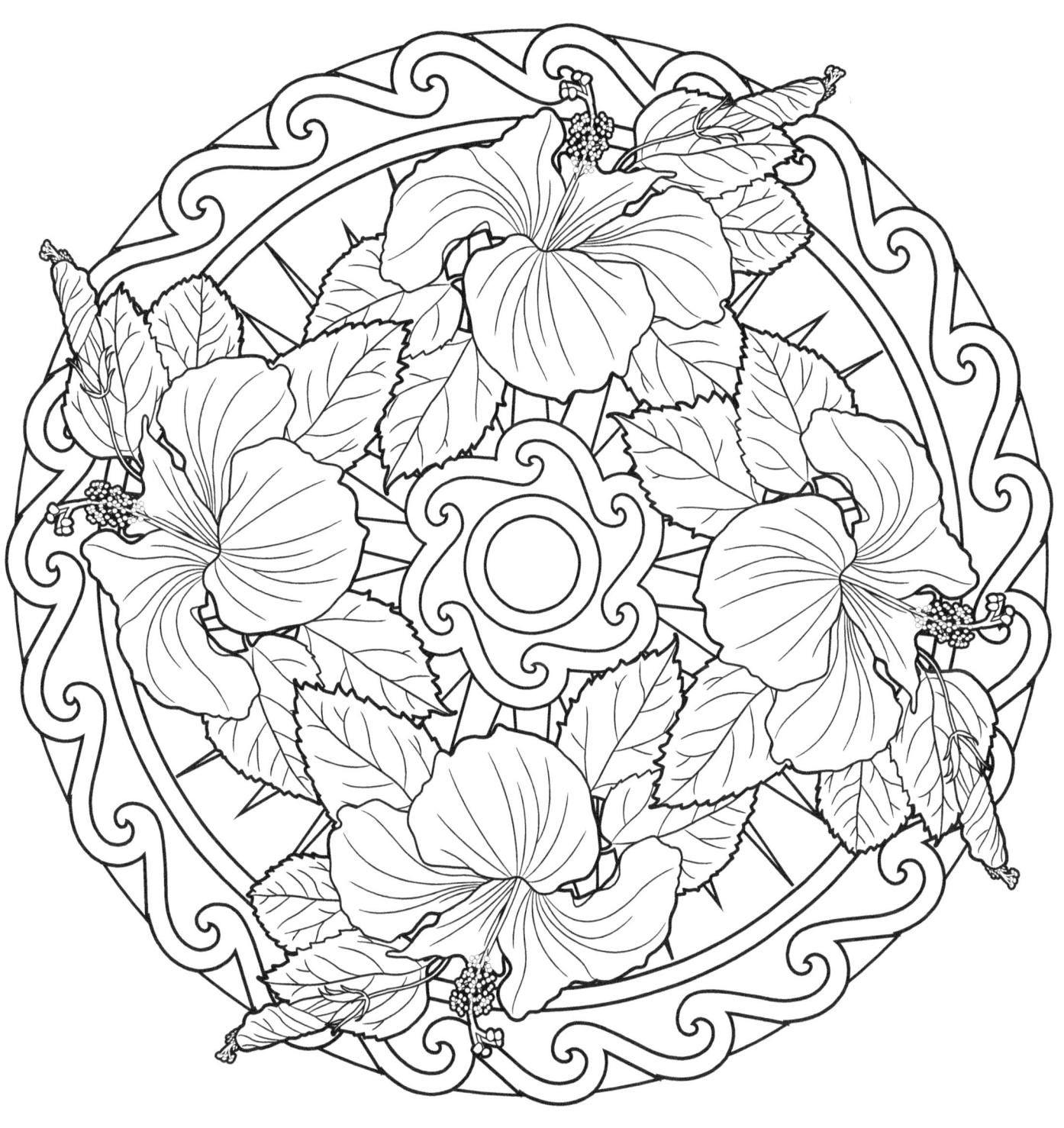

Hibiscus
Hibisceae

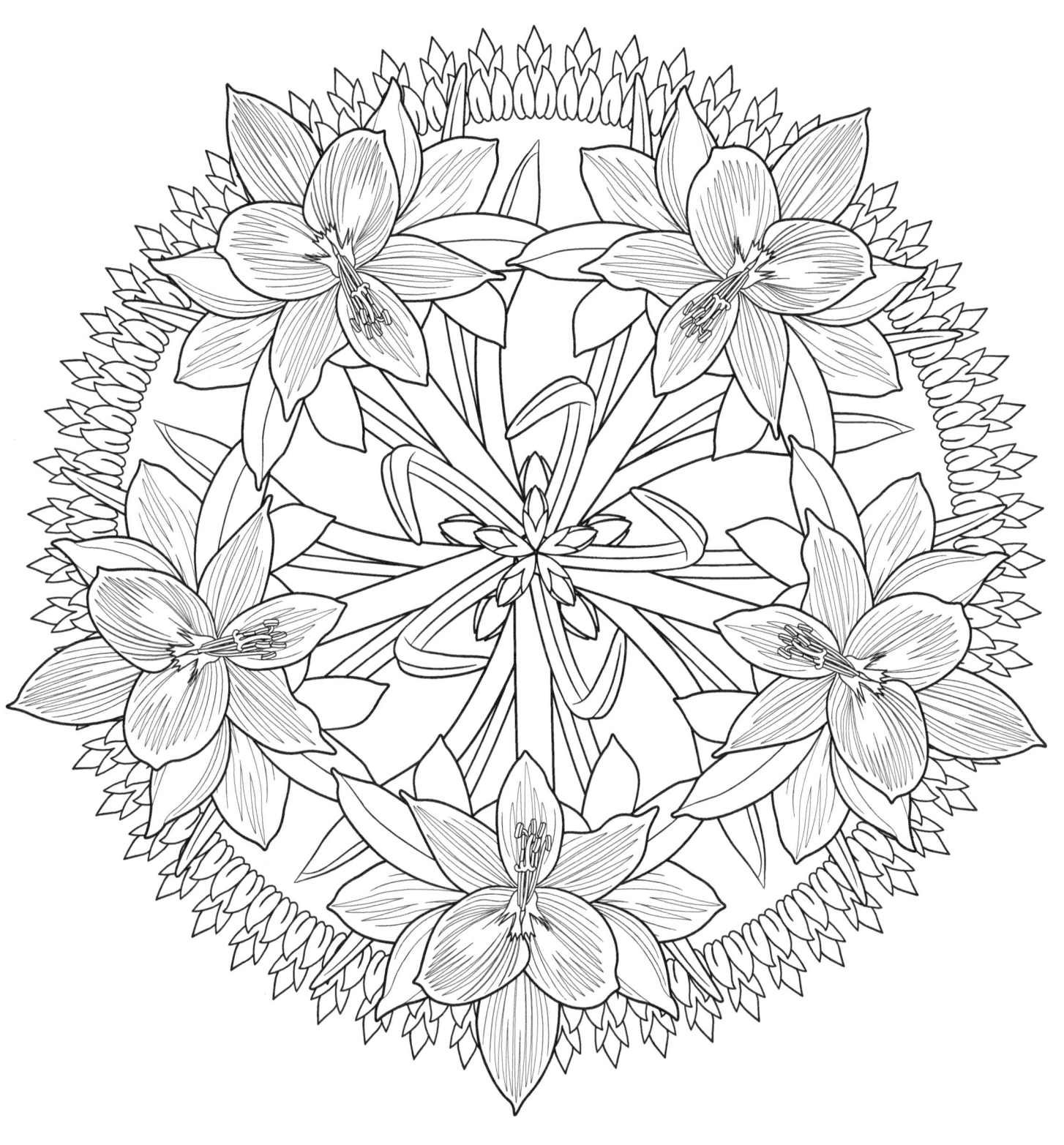

Knight's Star Lily
Hippeastrum

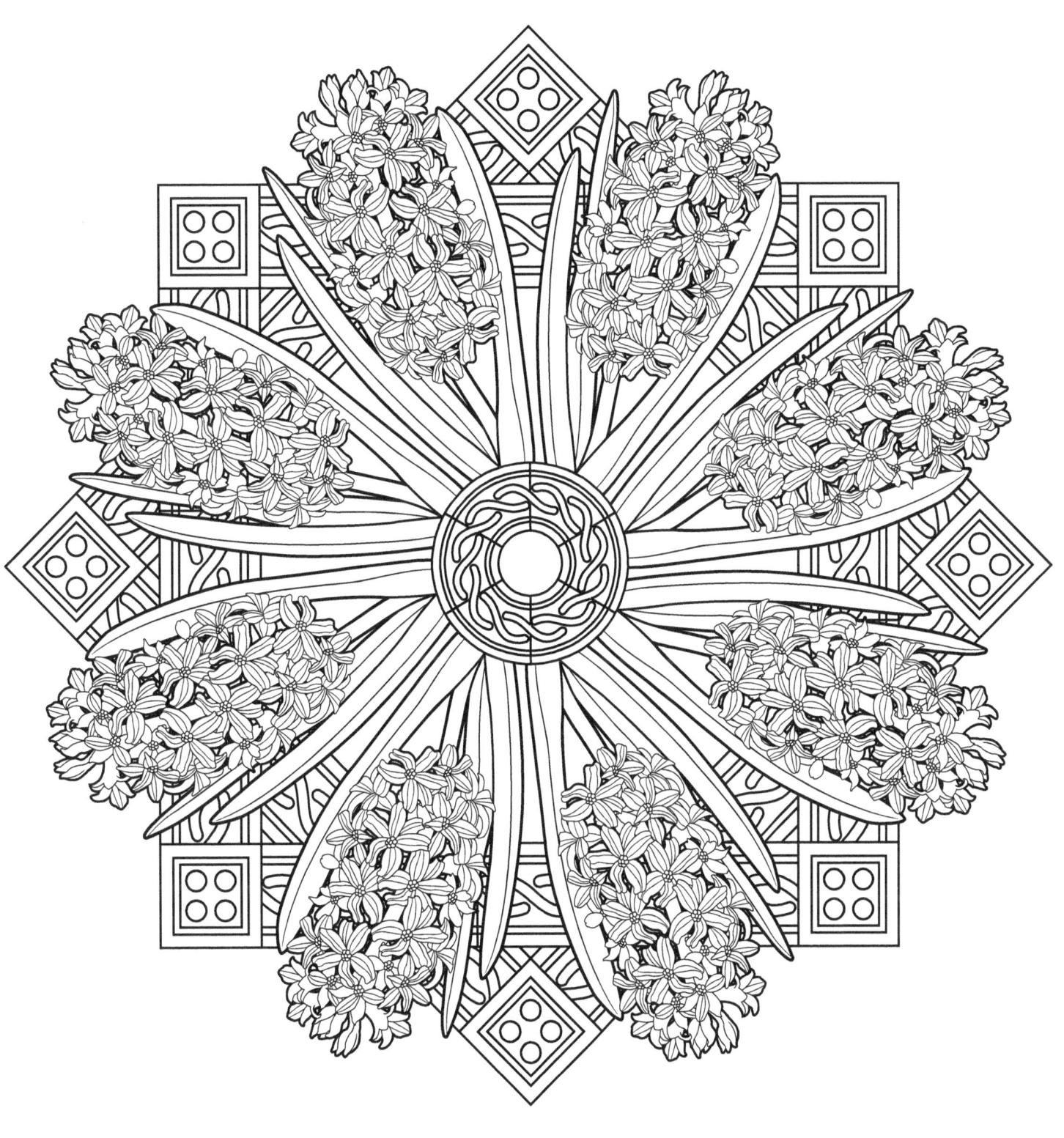

Hyacinth
Hyacinthus

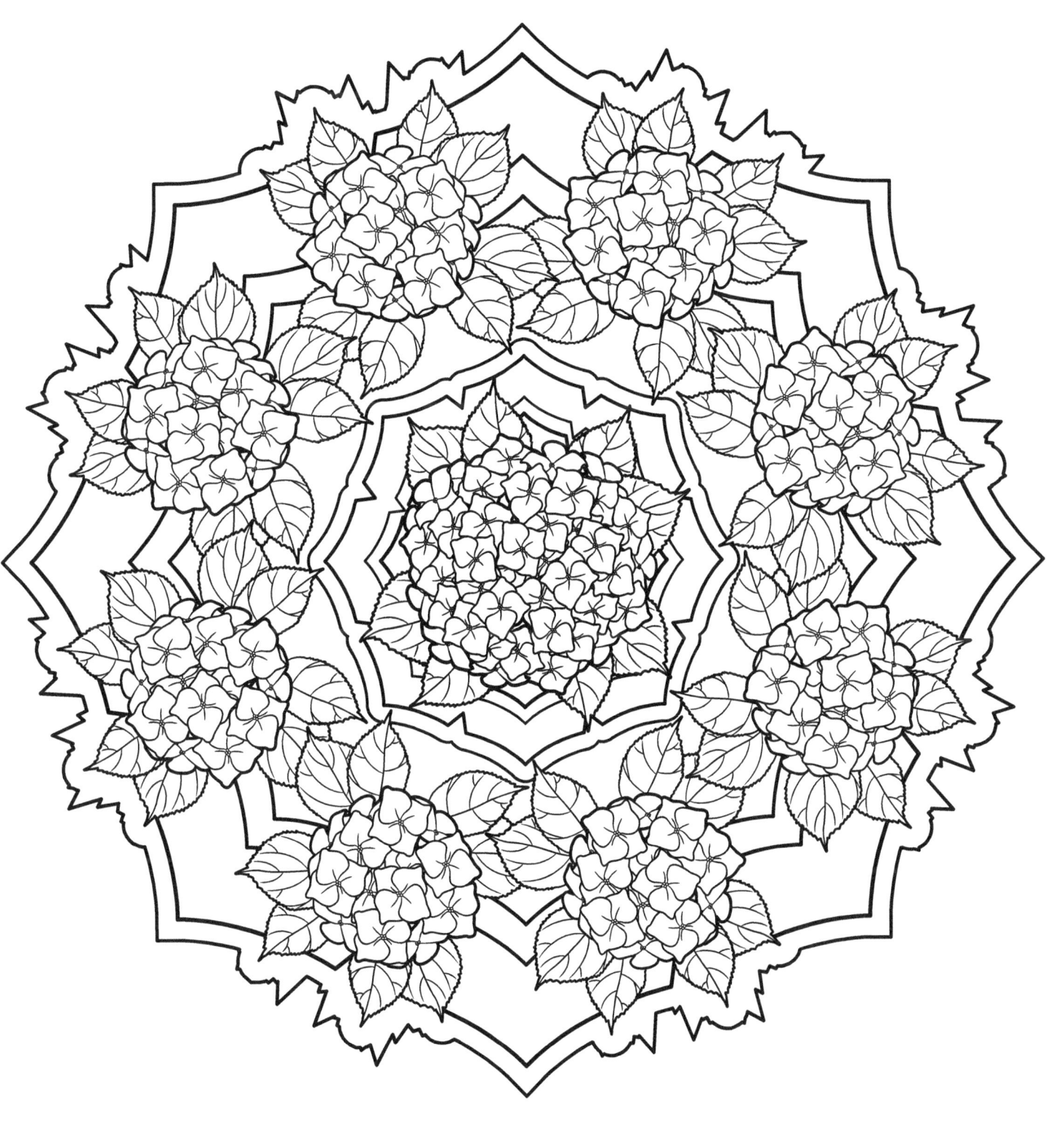

Hydrangea
Hydrangeaceae

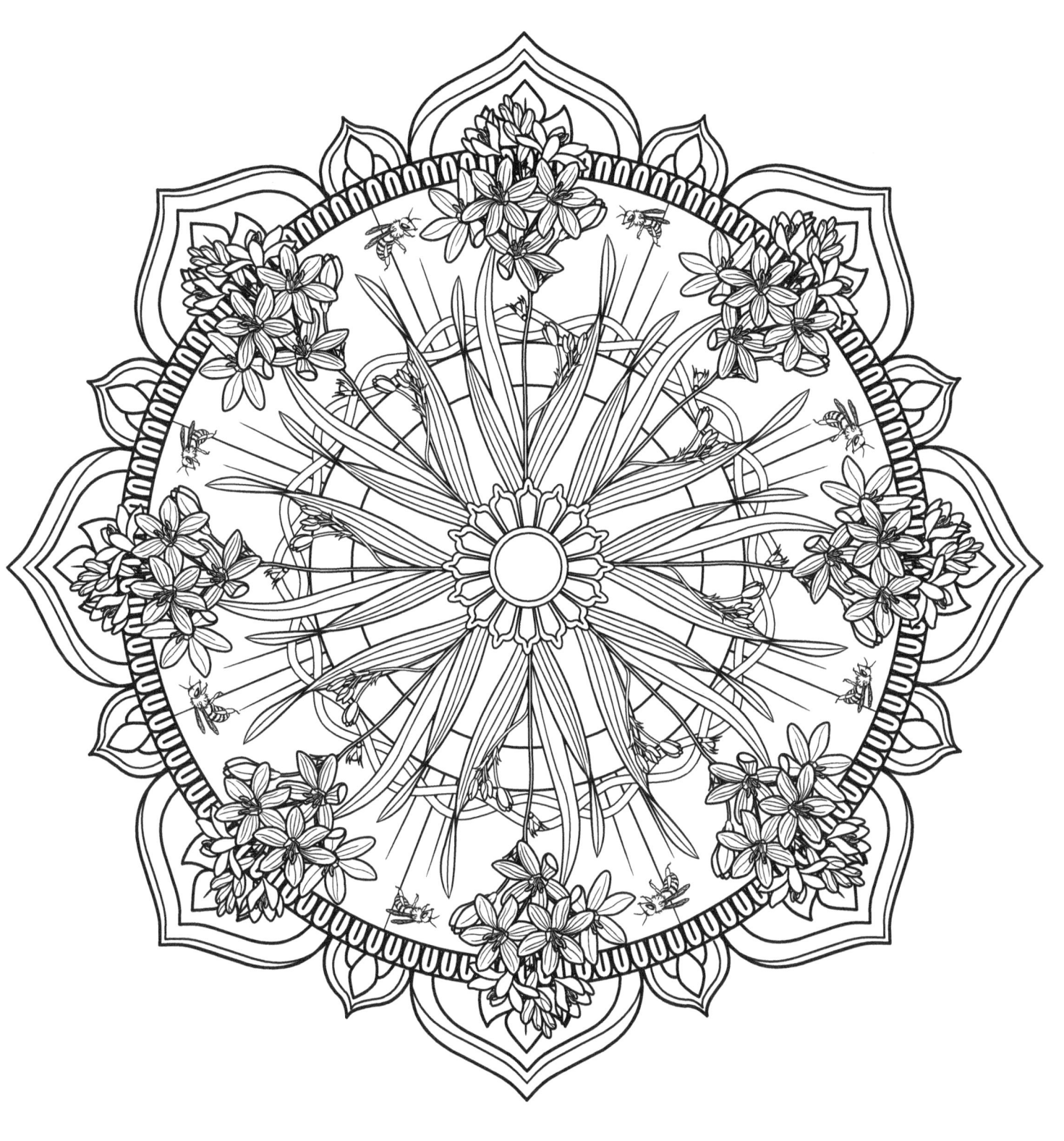

African Corn Lily
Ixia Longituba

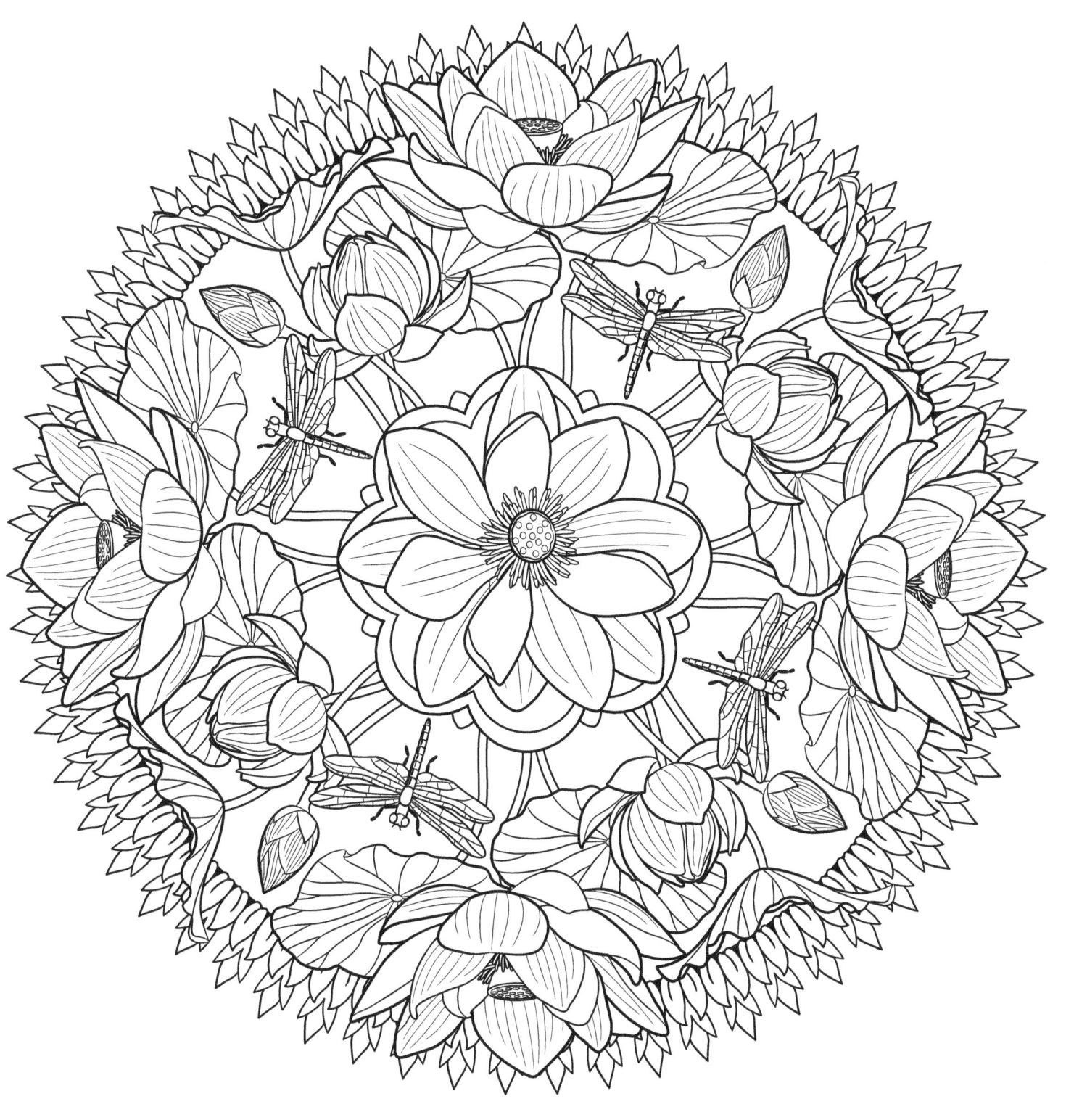

Lotus
Nelumbo nucifera

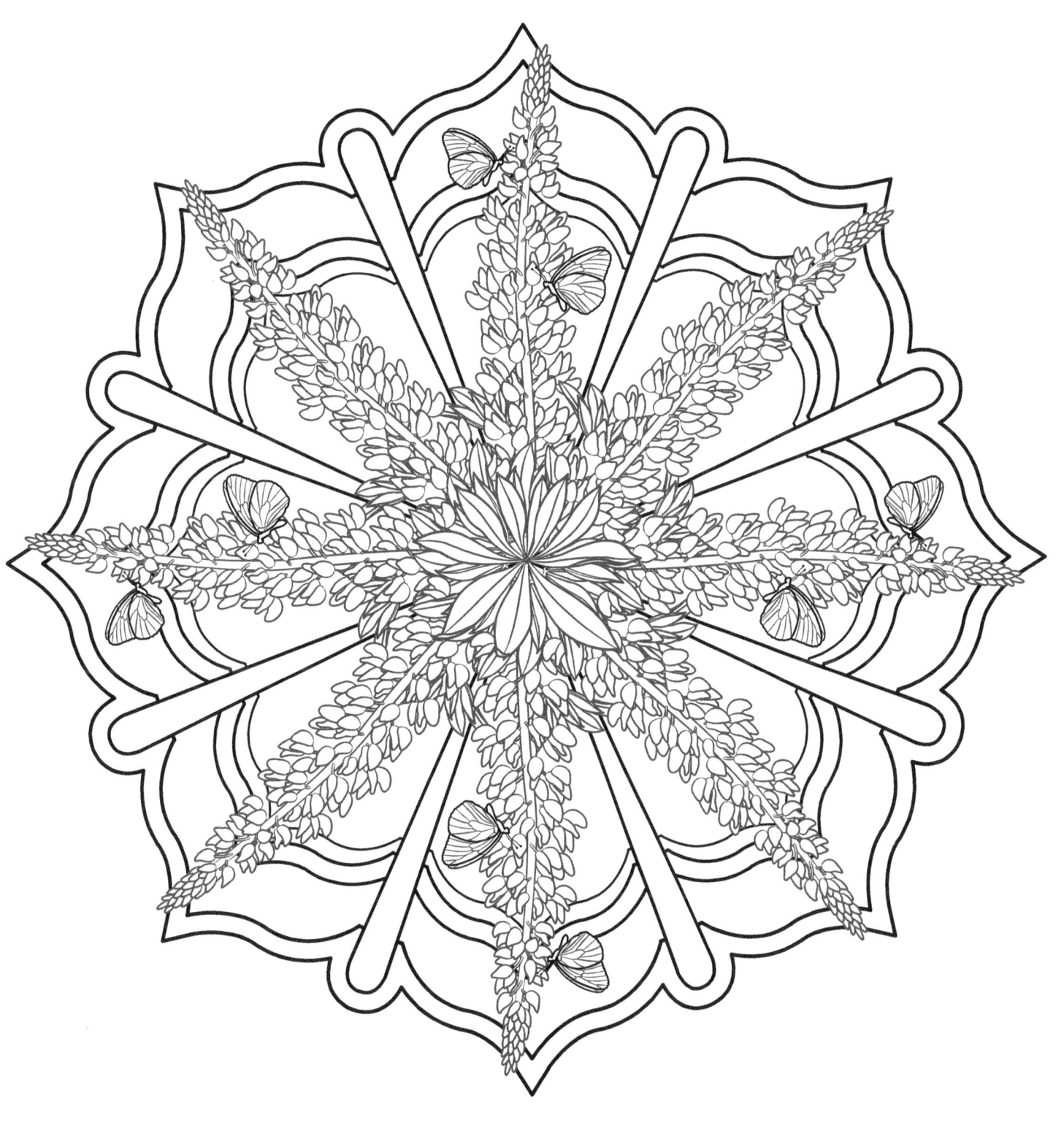

Lupine
Lupinus

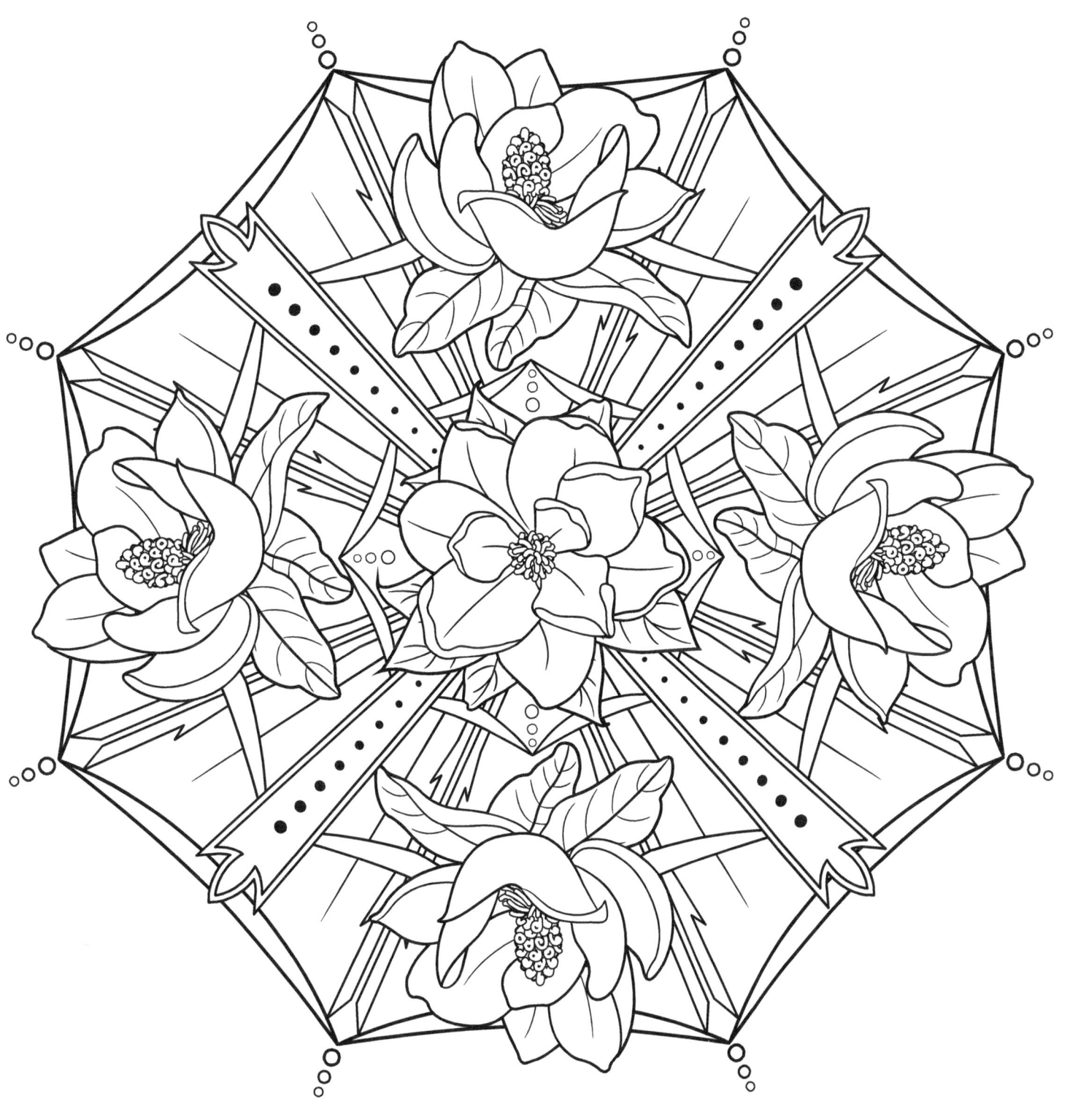

Magnolia
Magnoliaceae

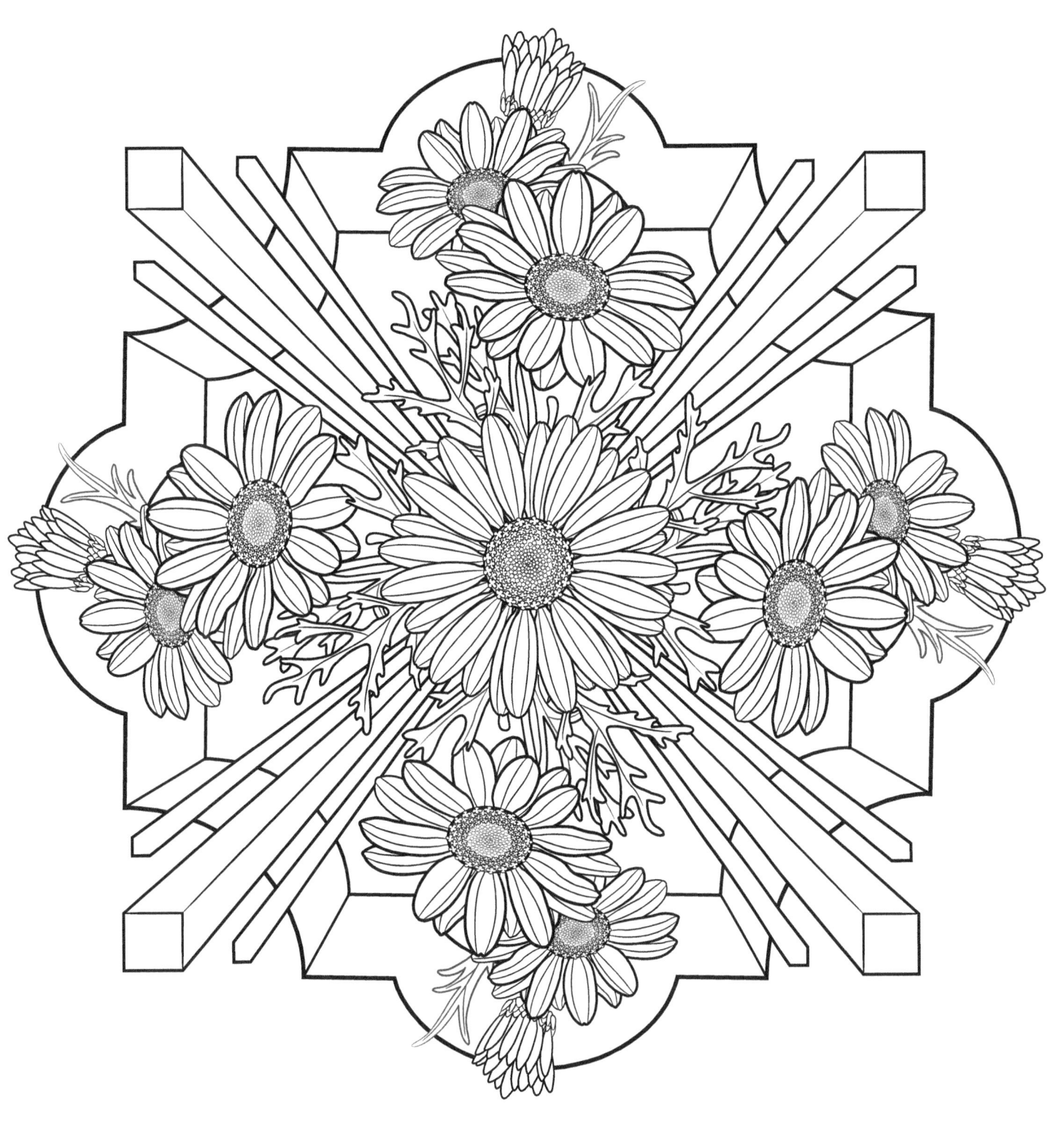

Marguerite Daisy
Argyranthemum frutescens

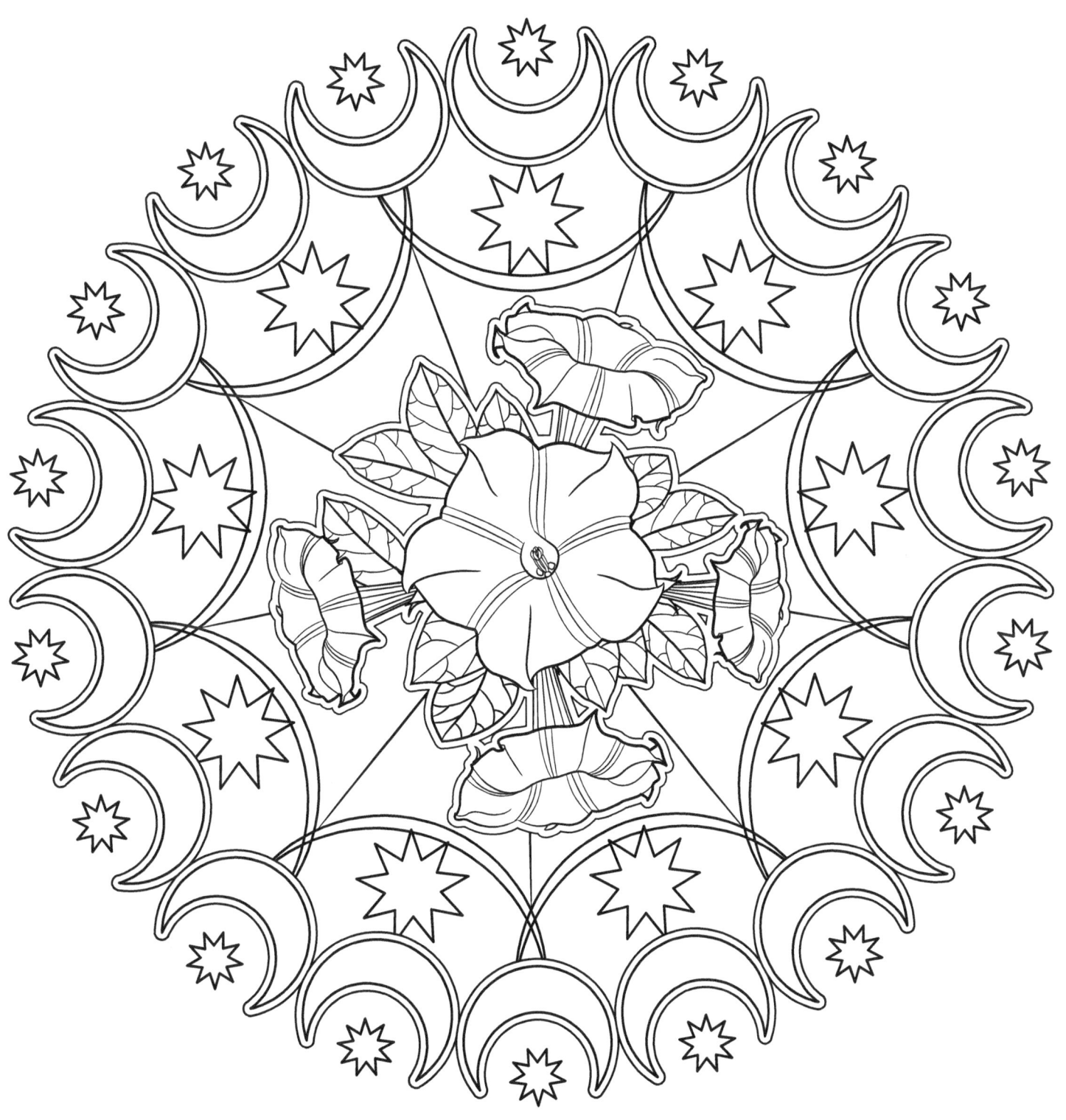

Moon Flower
Ipomoea

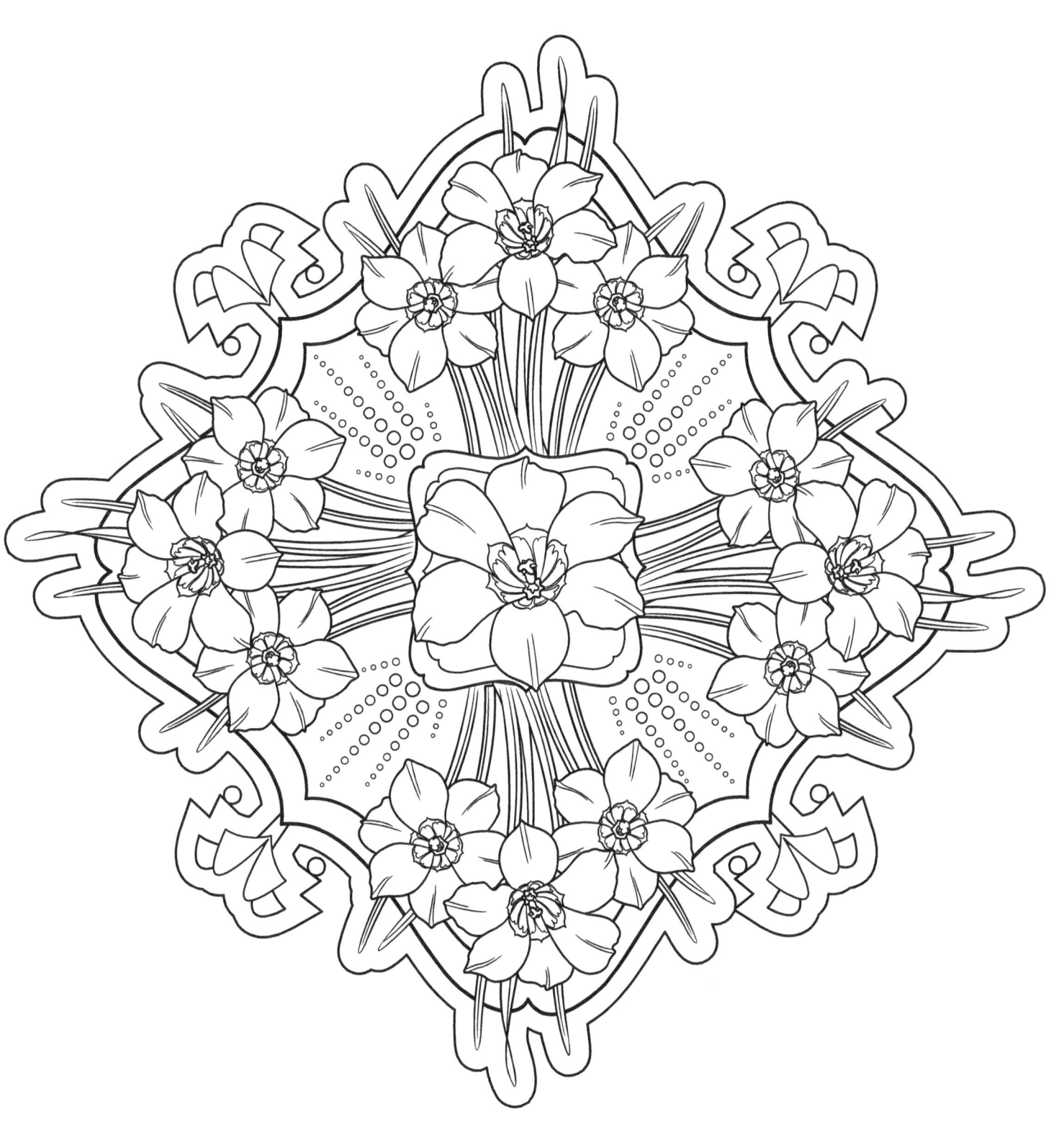

Moraea
Iridaceae

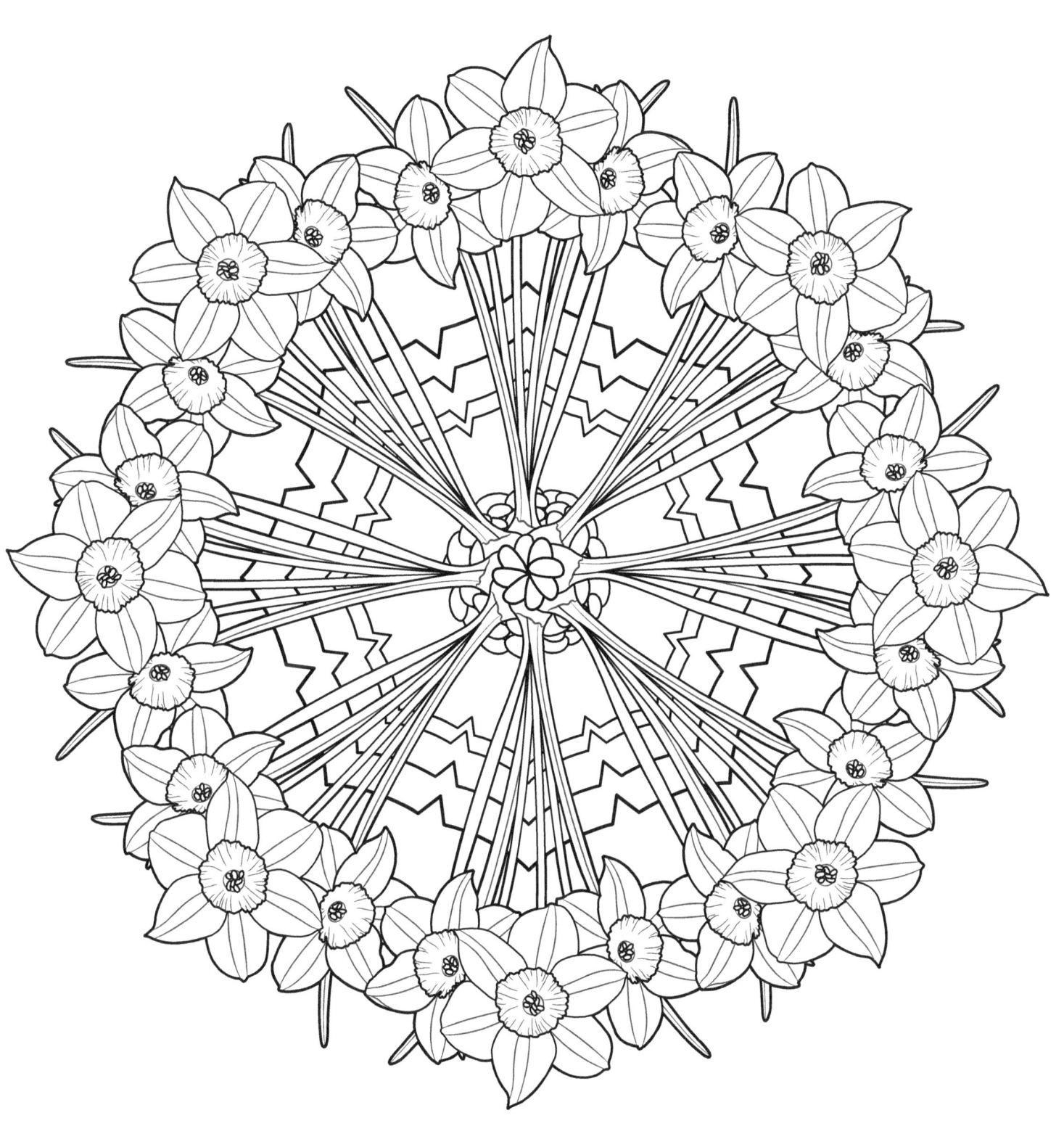

Daffodil
Narcissus

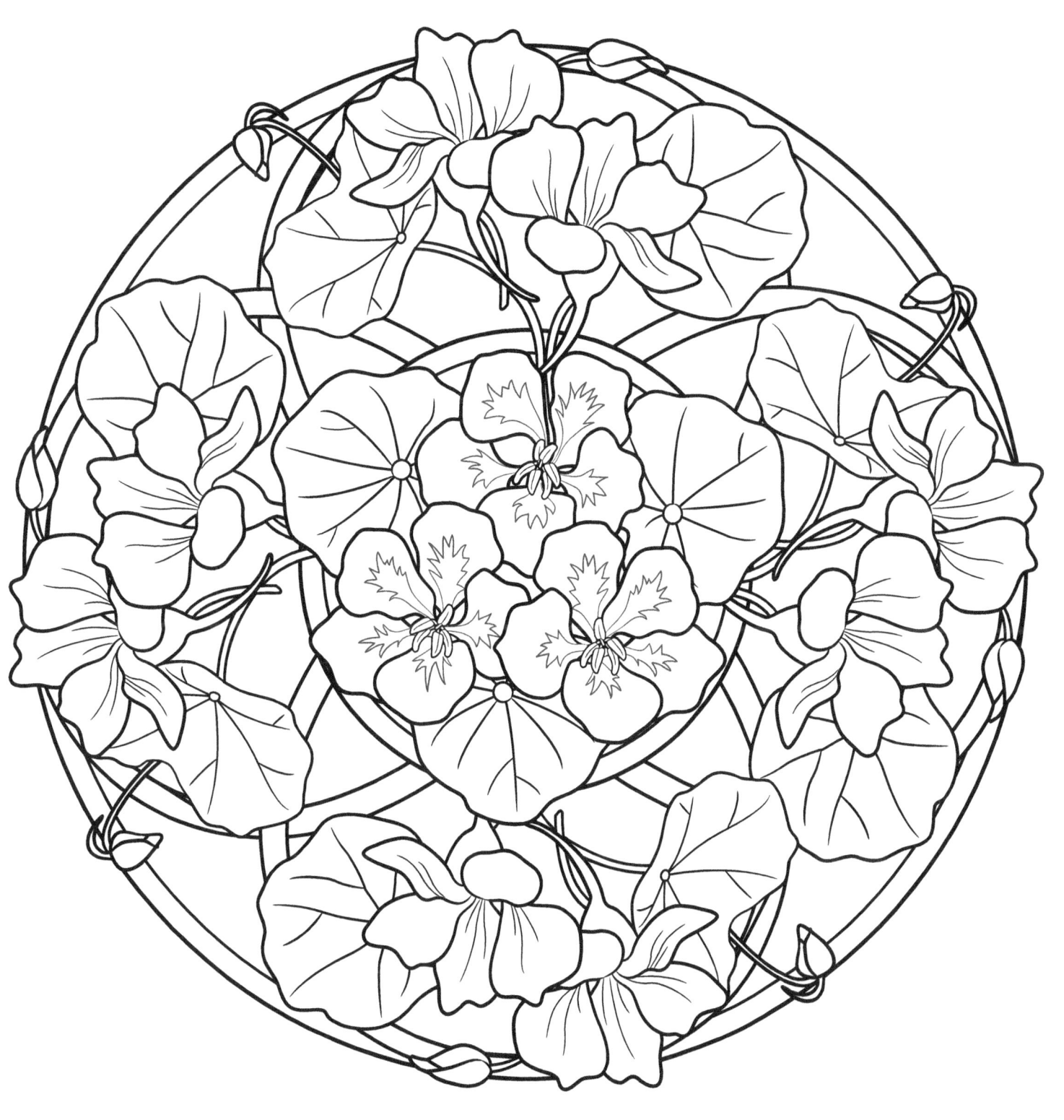

Nasturtium
Tropaeolum

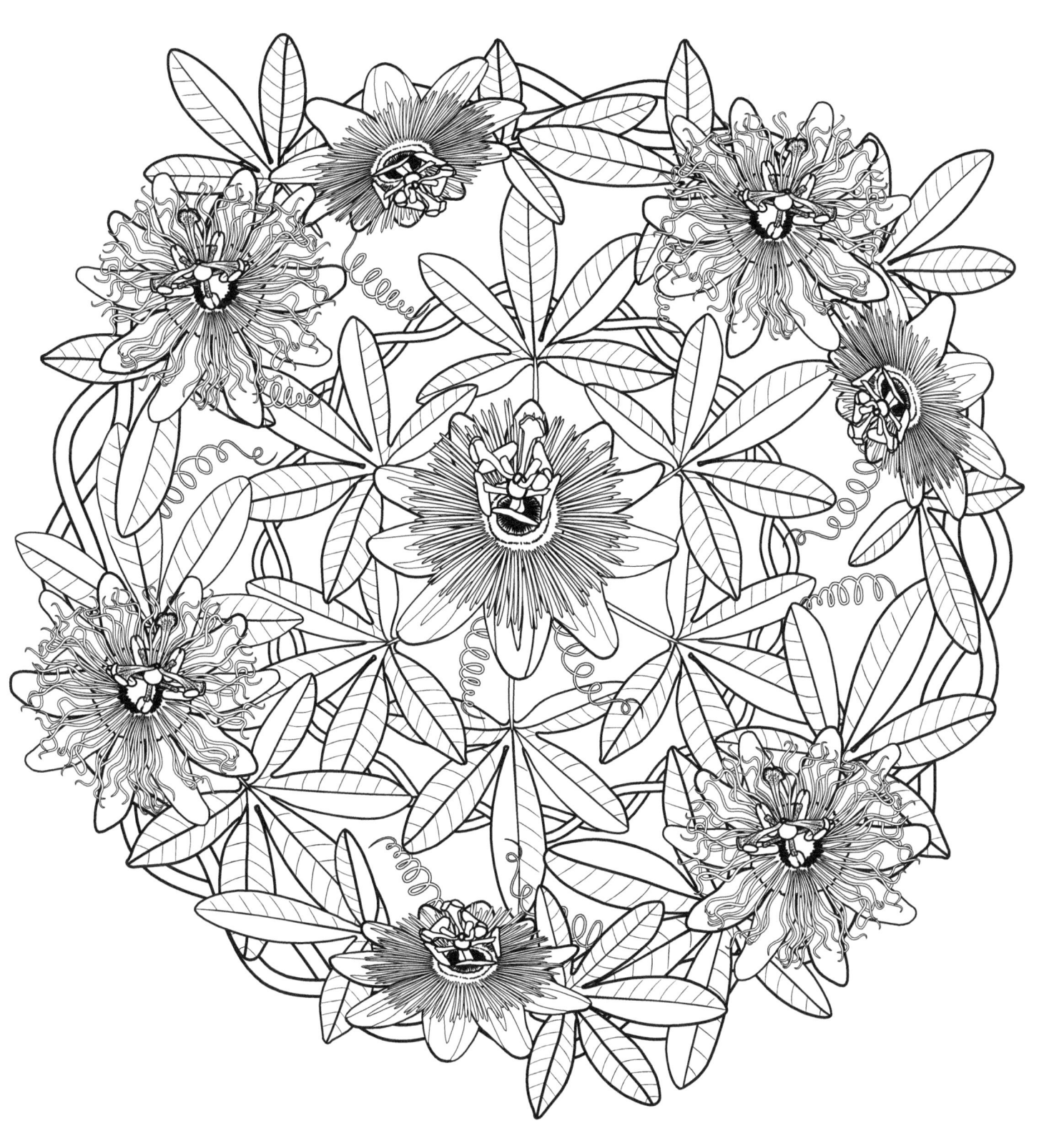

Passion Flower
Passifloraceae

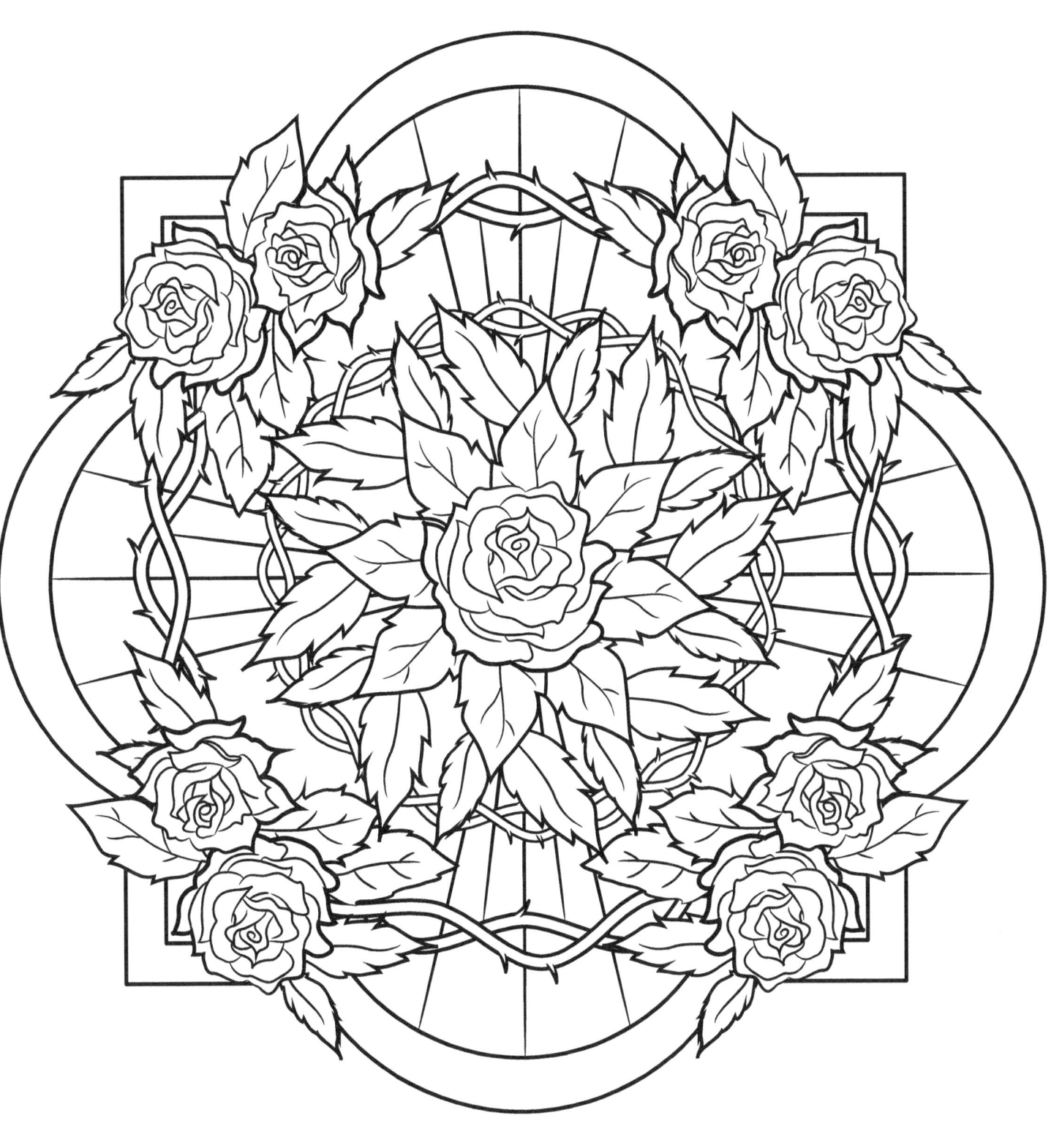

Rose
Rosaceae

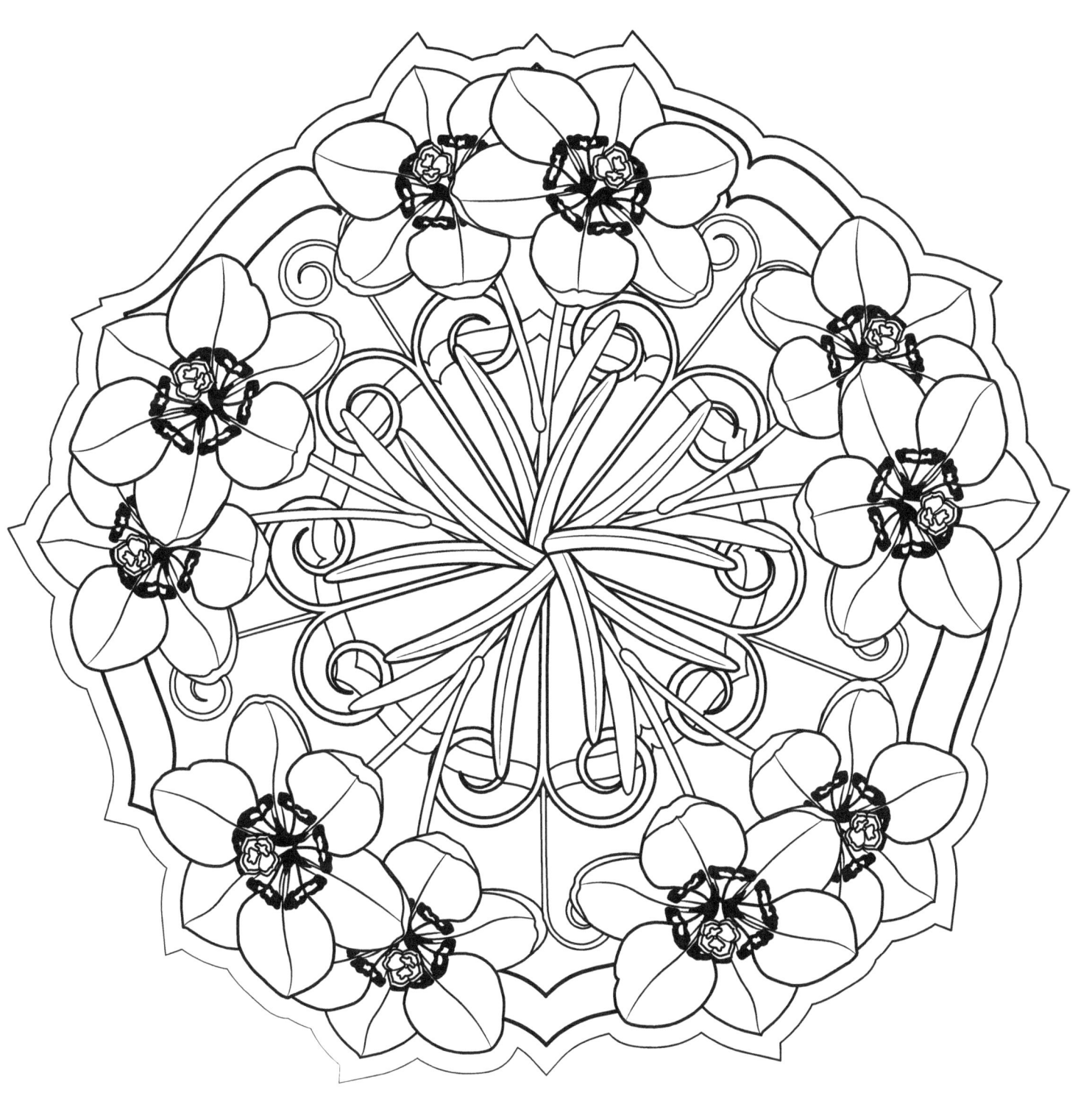

Harlequin Flower
Spraxix Elegans

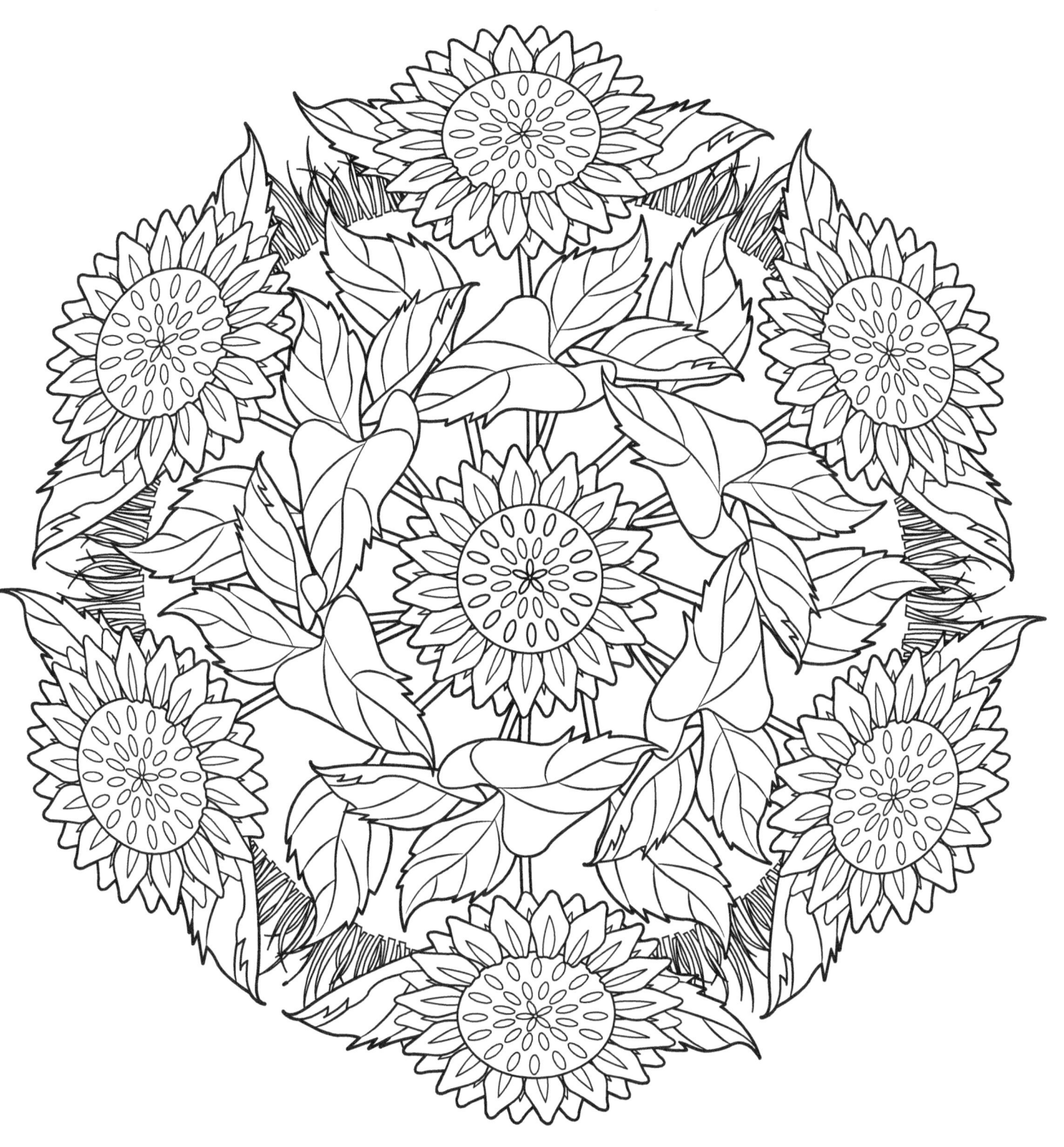

Sunflower
Helianthus

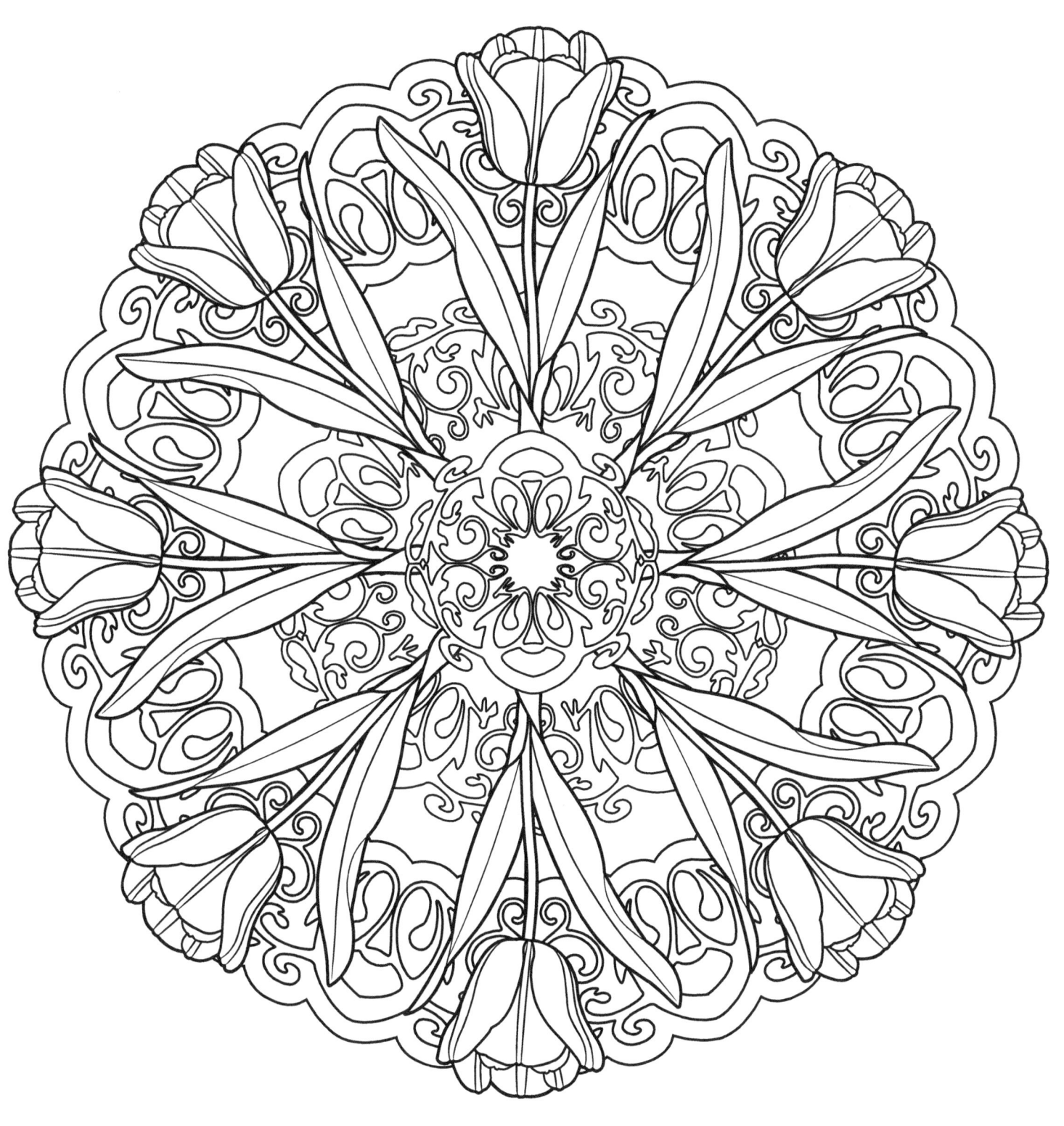

Tulip
Tulipa

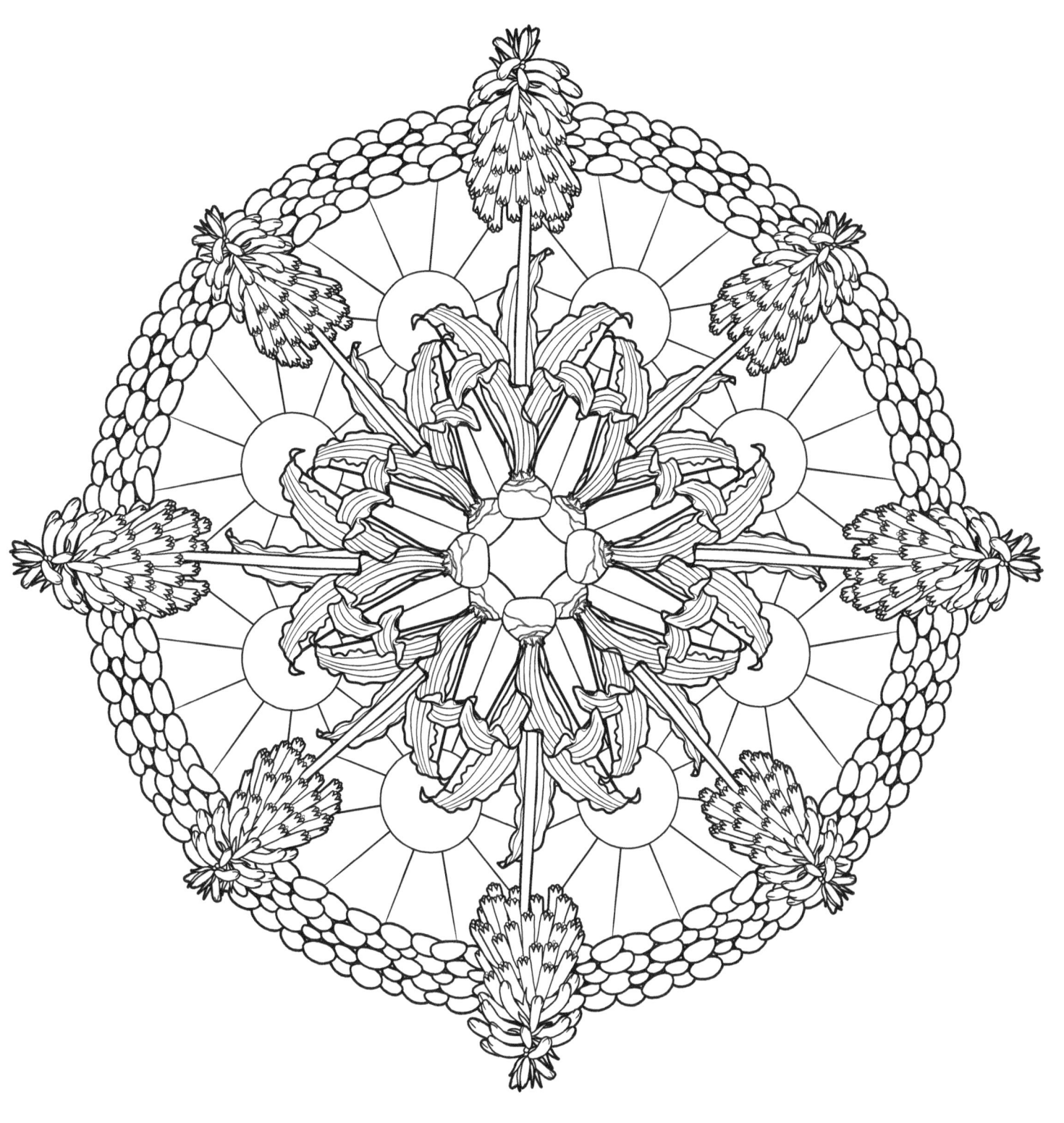

Forest Lily
Veltheimia Bracteata

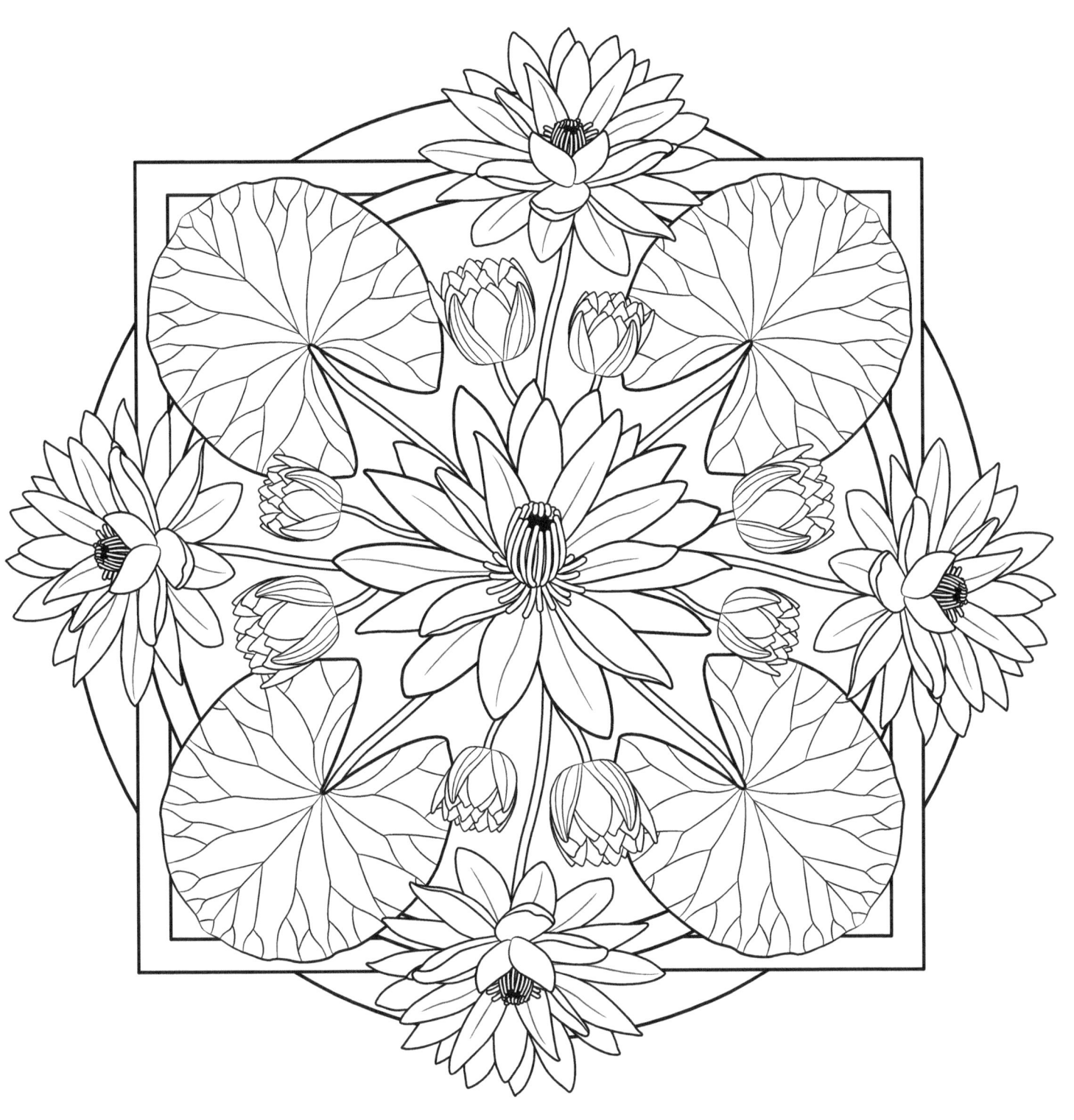

Waterlily
Nymphaea

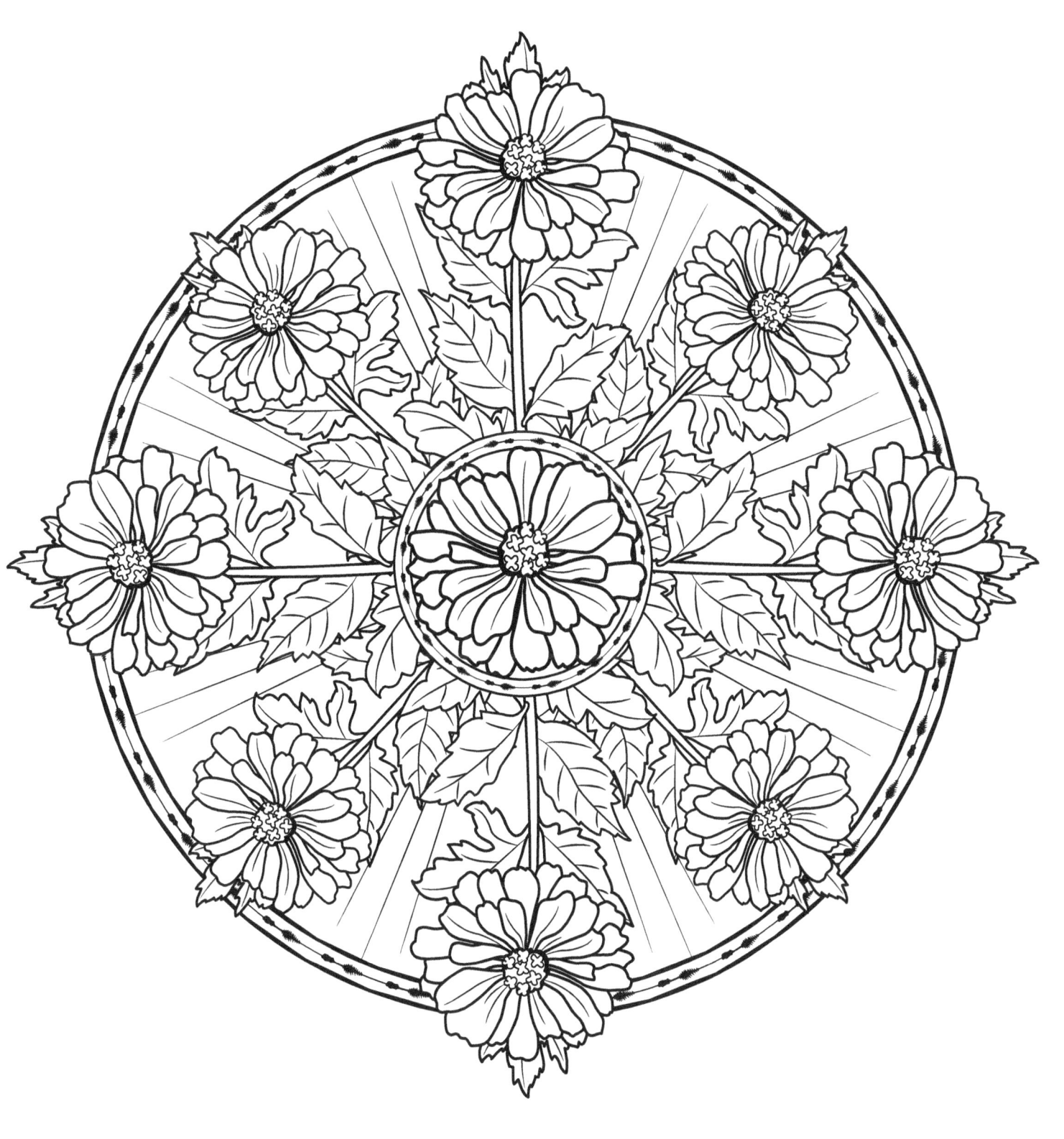

Zinnia
Zinnia Elegans

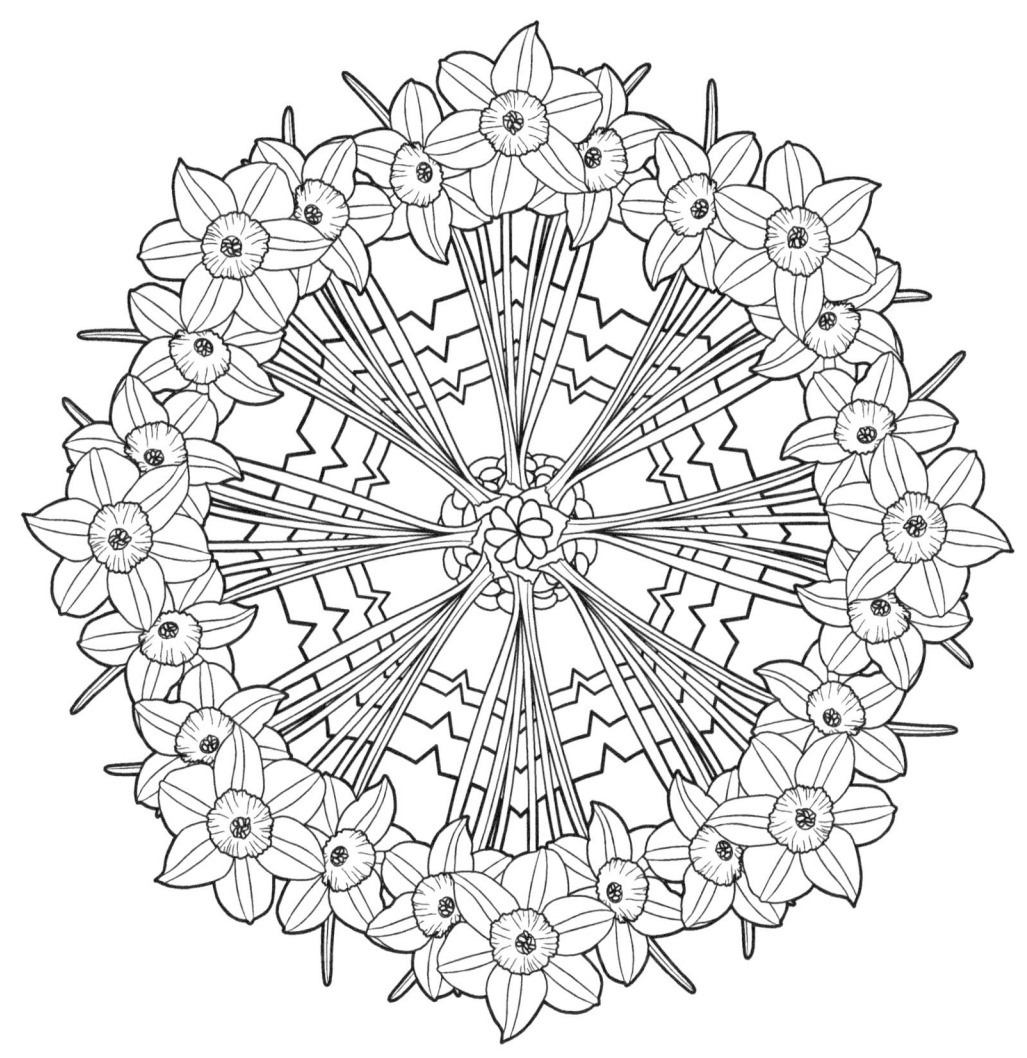

About The Artist

Pamela Duarte received a BFA from Art Center College of Design. After graduation she worked as a fashion illustrator and then segued into fashion dolls. She has worked on projects for many companies including Mattel Toys where she has illustrated Barbie and other products. She has also designed for toy companies in Hong Kong.
She loves to travel and has lived in Los Angeles, New York, and Bali. She currently lives in the peaceful Ojai Valley.

Other books by the Artist:

Flower Patterns Coloring Book, Volume 1

These illustrations are for personal use only.

www.ingramcontent.com/pod-product-compliance
Lightning Source LLC
Chambersburg PA
CBHW080606180526
45168CB00007B/2800